90-Day Devotional for Men

90-Day
Devotional
for Men

Deepen Your Faith in
Five Minutes a Day

RON EDMONDSON

ROCKRIDGE
PRESS

Interior and Cover Designer: Jay Dea
Art Producer: Michael Hardgrove
Editor: John Makowski
Production Editor: Matthew Burnett
Photography used under license from © iStockphoto.com.

ISBN: Print 978-1-64152-657-9
      eBook 978-1-64152-658-6
R0

I dedicate this book to my
two grown sons. They are the men
I want to be like someday. They
make me want to be a better man.

Contents

Introduction

Welcome to the *90-Day Devotional for Men*. My guess is you either received this as a gift, because someone thought you would enjoy it, or you picked it up yourself, because you thought it might be beneficial to you. Either way, I'm also guessing you're a man who genuinely wants to grow as a disciple of Christ. I love that. We share hearts in that matter. My greatest desire in life is to be found faithful and obedient to God.

I really believe we need more godly men in our churches and homes. I know firsthand the demands of society. I see all the stereotypes about men these days. I also know so many men who want to be spiritual leaders. They want to lead in their homes, churches, and workplaces, but they don't always know how. Frankly, many of our churches are lacking in good male mentoring and disciple-making.

And let's face it, you're busy. Every man I know is busy. The demands on your schedule seem to be mounting, not slowing down. As vital as you may feel it is, where is the time to develop yourself spiritually? Perhaps you need something that can provide a meaningful time with God each day, but which is also quick and easy enough to make sure you can complete it.

I started writing short devotionals years ago for that very reason. I was busy. Between my two boys' ball schedules, leading a growing—and sometimes not growing—business, serving at my church and in the community, and trying to be a decent husband, little time was left for personal study.

I figured there were others like me. I decided that spending a few minutes a day with God was better than missing the opportunity altogether. There would be days and seasons I could read, study, and pray longer, but I wanted to create a consistent daily routine. And I wanted to help others do the same.

If you can relate to any of that, you'll find that this book is designed with just that in mind. Each devotional is designed to be finished in five minutes or less. If you want to ponder further on a point or journal along the way, that's up to you.

The fact that this is a 90-day devotional is also intentional. It's a good length to help develop a healthy rhythm. You may form a routine and want to do another 90 days. Who knows? The habits might just stick. That would certainly be my prayer for you.

I've been in vocational ministry for 18 years and spent the first half of my career in the marketplace mostly as a self-employed business owner—my wife, Cheryl, and I once owned a business together. I served in an elective office in our community and was very active in our local church. Along the way, as I mentioned previously, I strived to find time to spend in God's Word. I was blessed enough to know the value of doing so. Daily devotionals were a huge help to me.

I would often share devotionals with a group of guys. We frequently did them together and discussed them over a weekly lunch. As I matured, I started inviting younger guys to join us on our devotionals. Looking back at my spiritual journey, having something I could do every day was a huge part of my discipleship.

You are not going to be blown away by the deep intellectual thoughts of this book. First, I'm not a deep intellectual. Second, that's not really the goal. Certainly, I want you to think, but more than that, I simply want you to be productive in God's Word every day.

And, again, something tells me you want that, too, or you likely wouldn't have kept reading this far. So, let's journey together.

Each day, I'll start with an opening verse of Scripture. I know we must keep all Scripture in context, so if the verse feels out of context, I'll try to explain (you can always read the full passage from which the verse was taken on days where you have more time, or go back later). Then, I'll expand upon the idea in the verse. Sometimes, I'll share some personal stories to help illustrate. I share many stories about raising my boys because that process taught me a lot about God. I'll close with a suggested prayer, and then give you a moment for some reflection. There will be some space where you can write down any quick thoughts, such as things you are thankful for, prayer requests, or some idea you want to come back to later. I find that writing something down always helps me remember and apply it.

That's it. Pretty simple. Let's get started.

The
Devotionals

1 Watch Out for Naysayers

When Eliab, David's oldest brother, heard him speaking with the men, he burned with anger at him and asked, "Why have you come down here? And with whom did you leave those few sheep in the wilderness? I know how conceited you are and how wicked your heart is; you came down only to watch the battle."

—1 SAMUEL 17:28 NIV

"You'll never be successful that way. Why don't you give up?" "That won't work. You're just wasting your time." "We've never done it that way before."

Have you ever met a naysayer? What about a dream killer? I don't know about you, but I have met plenty of them. They are the ones who love to kill a deal. They are always thinking of reasons why something shouldn't work. I have often thought that if they spent half as much time working toward a goal as they do criticizing it, they would probably accomplish more than the average person! I base that on the fact that they can certainly be successful at stopping progress at times.

Now, I am not speaking against godly wisdom. I have had people I trust, who have prayed through a situation, help me reconsider one of my ideas. Their wisdom turned out to be best for me. I depend on my wife for that kind of support. If I run a suggestion by her and, after prayer, she disagrees, I see it as a good indication that I shouldn't go forward with it.

I'm talking about those who just can't look on the bright side of any issue. They always see the negative instead of the positive. They love to stop a dream by pointing out all the things that could go wrong.

David's brothers responded to him that way when he came to fight Goliath. What if he had listened to the naysayers?

Watch out for the naysayers in life. And, don't be afraid to chase a dream. Check it out with God's Word first. If He says it is okay, then *go for it*!

Prayer: God, help me stand against the negative voices today.

Reflect: Spend some time today thinking of all that has been accomplished in this world that would have been stopped if people had listened to the critics. Would Noah have built the ark? Would Peter have gotten out of the boat? Would we have cars or telephones or computers?

2 Godly Fathers

The living, the living—they praise you, as I am doing today; parents tell their children about your faithfulness.

—ISAIAH 38:19 NIV

Godly fathers testify to the goodness of God.

When my boys were still at home, they loved to hear me tell stories of my past. There were certain stories, mostly about trials we had endured by God's grace, that I was asked to tell over and over again. I think they loved being reminded of God's goodness to our family.

A godly father also tells his children about his journey with the Lord. Of course, one can't tell of his journey with the Lord unless he has one. So, a godly father has a consistent, growing relationship with Christ.

But a godly father doesn't keep the goodness of God to himself. He shares it with his children.

In biblical days, fathers spent many hours teaching their children about the customs of the people and the laws of God. Sure, times were different then, and many men worked near their homes and with their children.

I wonder, though: Do our children need our instruction any less today? I would suggest not. Our children need us to share with them the goodness of God as we have learned of it from personal experience.

A godly heritage is passed on through godly men who share godliness with their children on a consistent basis. Are you passing on a godly heritage?

Prayer: God, prompt me to share the good You've brought into my life with my children and others.
Reflect: Spend some time thinking about all God has done in your life. Have you ever felt His presence in a very real way? Has there been a time when you felt all hope was lost, but God came through for you? Can you remember one good thing that happened to you that you knew had to be "a God thing"? Then, ask yourself: Have I ever shared these things with others? Have I shared them with my children?

3 Leaving a Legacy

Godly men buried Stephen and mourned deeply for him.

—ACTS 8:2 NIV

Perhaps you know the story of Stephen, one of the greatest Christian martyrs of the early church. Stephen was not ashamed of the Gospel. In the seventh chapter of Acts, he preached one of the greatest sermons in the New Testament.

Stephen reminded the Sanhedrin, the ancient legal court of Jewish elders, how God called Abraham to go to a land he could not see. He spoke of Moses and the deliverance of the Israelites from Egypt. He also told of Jesus, the prophesied Messiah, who had come to save His people from their sins. Finally, Stephen told them that they were the ones who sentenced Jesus to death on the Cross.

His words were powerful, direct, and true. It was a toe-stomping, finger-pointing, shoe-fitting delivery of the Gospel. The Sanhedrin was not pleased. Immediately, they began to stone Stephen, killing him.

Stephen stood firm, however, even praising God amid the brutality as he died. What a testimony!

Stephen was a godly man. He lived his life with a faith that allowed him to finish strong. Stephen probably didn't leave this earth the way he might have wanted, but he finished well with his God.

Godly men mourned Stephen because Stephen was a godly man.

Who will be the godly men who mourn for you?

Please understand, I'm not asking if you have a clean record. It's probably too late for that now, isn't it? It is too late for all of us. That's why we need a Savior.

I'm asking if you have a willing heart, a heart that says, "God, here I am, take my life and do with it what You will." I suspect that was the way Stephen lived his life.

Make it your aim to finish strong so that godly men will mourn for you.

Prayer: God, help me live my life in a way that godly men will truly mourn for me someday.

Reflect: Spend a few minutes today reflecting on your legacy. What will it be? What will people say about you? What will people remember? More important, what will God say about you?

4 Choose *Joy* Today!

Whatever happens, dear friends, be glad in the Lord. I never get tired of telling you this, and it is good for you to hear it again and again.

—PHILIPPIANS 3:1 TLB

Philippians is a letter about joy, written to an early church in the Greek city of Philippi. The author, Paul, shares joy throughout his letter. Each of us is to strive for joy.

Paul wrote to the members of this church as if he was their father, and, in a spiritual sense, he was like a father to them. His insistent tone makes me think he was telling them something he knew they wouldn't instantly embrace as truth. It's something he knew he would have to say to them often.

If you are a father, you most likely know what it's like to try to give your children wisdom, even when you know they probably won't receive it as such at the time. But your job is to share your wisdom and experiences with them, and so you do, often repeating the same things over and over again.

Paul had learned that the Lord desires to give His children joy, even when life doesn't appear to be quite so en-*joy*-able. Paul knew that it would be best for believers if they would choose joy, even when trials kept life from being "fun."

Christians can have joy in life, not based on circumstances in the world, but based on the condition of their relationship with Christ. They can be joyful in the hope of eternity. As followers of Christ, we know it all ends well. That should be a motivating factor toward consistent joy.

I'm still very much on the receiving end of Paul's advice. I need this reminder daily. I'm learning more every day, though, that joy really is achievable, even throughout the storms of life.

Let's be students of Paul today and choose the joy we have in Jesus Christ!

Prayer: Lord, whatever comes my way today, help me choose joy.

Reflect: Before you end the day, spend a few minutes reflecting on the things in life that bring you joy. Don't neglect to remember your salvation and the eternal rewards you've been guaranteed by Christ to inherit.

5 Let People See Who You Are

By their fruit you will recognize them. Do people pick grapes from thornbushes, or figs from thistles?

—MATTHEW 7:16 NIV

Jesus had a way of speaking very clearly and sometimes rather bluntly.

I am not a tree expert, but I am fascinated with people who are. They can not only identify an oak tree, but they can tell me exactly what type of oak it is. Can you tell the difference between an English Sycamore and an American Sycamore? Do their "accents" set them apart?

We once had a neighbor who had a tree full of apples. I love a nice, shiny red or green apple picked fresh off the tree (and I love the apple pies made with them, too). I must be honest, however; I couldn't have told you what kind of tree they'd come from unless I had seen it when it was loaded with fruit. For most of the year, it looked just like any other tree.

You understand why, don't you? I needed to see its fruit first. Frankly, I can't tell an apple tree from a pear tree without first looking at its fruit.

Are you a Christian? I hope you are! Only you and God know for sure, but Jesus did give us a good indicator. He said we will be known by our fruit.

A follower of Christ should be the one who has patience while waiting in the slow lines at the supermarket. A Christian should be the one who doesn't stiff the waitstaff of a tip just because they forgot to refill your tea. A Christian should be the one who opens his or her door to those in need and gives to others, expecting nothing in return. A Christian should be the one in the office who refuses to participate in gossip, who forgives those who mistreat them, and exudes the love of Christ. Do you get the general idea?

I always had to wait for fall before I could know for sure that the tree in my neighborhood was going to bear apples each year. You and I, the children of God, however, should be in full bloom all year long.

Will others know what kind of "tree" you are today?

Prayer: Lord, help me bear fruit today that reflects who You are and who I am in You.

Reflect: Think about how others have been viewing you lately—your family, friends, coworkers, and those you simply meet on the street. Consider whether they would view you as a "fruit-bearing" child of God.

6 Put Away Childishness

When I was a child, I spoke like a child, I thought like a child, I reasoned like a child. When I became a man, I put aside childish things.

—1 CORINTHIANS 13:11 CSB

Paul makes the point that, as believers, we should be maturing. Discipleship means that we are becoming more like Christ, which implies that we are growing. Encouraging Christian maturity is a huge purpose of the church.

When I think of this verse, however, I'm always conflicted. Yes, I agree with Paul. When I became a man, I had to put aside childish things. I shouldn't pout when things don't go my way. I had to learn to forgive and refuse to hold a grudge. I must be willing to press through my fears in order to walk by faith. I must love people even when they may not return my love. That's all part of being a mature follower of Christ.

But two truths from Scripture must complement and not contradict each other. In Matthew 18:3 NIV, Jesus said, "Truly I tell you, unless you change and become like little children, you will never enter the kingdom of heaven."

Paul said to put away childish things, but Jesus seems to say we should take on childish things. Where is the balance of these two truths?

Of course, all Scripture is true, so there must be a reconciliation here somewhere.

Here is my takeaway:

In matters of trust—think like a child.
In matters of faith—behave like a child.
In matters of hope—trust like a child.

Our God is worthy of our trust, faith, and hope. Nothing that comes in my life will ever interfere with His plans or promises for me.

But at the same time, children can also be selfish. Part of a parent's job is to teach them not to be. Children can tell a lie to get out of trouble. A good parent disciplines them for this. Children can be lazy. They require structure to fulfill their responsibilities.

So, in matters of discipline and obedience, I must put away childish things.

I think the balance comes in who I am in Christ, which is a child of God, and how I am as I relate to others and in obedience to God. I must put away childishness.

Prayer: Lord, help me be mature in my obedience, but help me continually trust You like a child.
Reflect: In what areas of your life do you need to "put aside childish things"?

7 Send Someone Else

"Please, Lord, send someone else."

I love the raw, real, personal dialogue between Moses and God in Exodus 4. God told Moses to "Go to Egypt." He would be God's representative to lead the people out of slavery and to the Promised Land. But Moses had a few reservations. He was not gifted in speech. He didn't feel qualified.

Lovingly and patiently, God performed some miracles for Moses to witness His power. God promised He would be with Moses wherever he went (I would like to think all this would have been enough to convince me, but I realize this is probably not the case). With all the excuses, God never budged from the call He had placed on Moses's life.

So, after all the dialogue, Moses said something I've said so many times to God: "Please, Lord, send someone else." In other words, "Can you just let someone else do it, God, because I really don't want it to be me."

Love it! Thank you for your honesty, Moses. It's refreshing.

Have you ever wished God would send someone else? I would love my faith to be like Isaiah's when he said to the Lord, "Here I am. Send me" (Isaiah 6:8 CSB), or like Abraham, who got up in the morning and did what God told him to do (Genesis 22 CSB). Or Noah, who "did

14 90-Day Devotional for Men

everything that God had commanded him" (Genesis 6:22 CSB). Of course, each of them also had their own moments of doubt.

We know Moses was also capable of tremendous faith, as we see in the rest of his story, but I am reminded that Moses was human, too. He was capable of genuine doubt and resistance to God's plan for his life. And I'm also reminded that I am often like Moses was at the beginning of his journey. I would love God to send someone else. Faith-walking is never easy.

What can we learn from this? It affirms for me that if God is calling us to something bigger than we feel able to do, we should not be surprised when our emotions try to talk us (and God) out of it. Luckily, God is never wavered by our human frailties.

Prayer: God, thank You for believing in me, even when I can't seem to believe in myself.

Reflect: Think for a moment about what God may have for you to do that you don't feel prepared or equipped to do. Then, ask yourself if you can trust Him as Moses had to.

8 Listening for the Father's Approval

The master was full of praise. "Well done, my good and faithful servant. You have been faithful in handling this small amount, so now I will give you many more responsibilities. Let's celebrate together!"

—MATTHEW 25:21 NLT

Those are the words that all believers long to hear. Amen!

I don't know about you, but I want to hear my Father's approval someday. When my life's story is over on this earth, I want to enter His presence and hear that He is pleased with how I lived my life.

In fact, I want to know He approves of me even today. Sometimes, I reflect and wonder if He is truly pleased with my life and progress. I want to know that my God calls me faithful.

When my sons were still living at home, I would often look into their eyes and be reminded that they wanted the same from me. Once, I went to the elementary school to have lunch with our 10-year-old son, and the first thing he said to me as we sat down at the table was how well he had done on a spelling test that morning. He wanted my approval. And he got it.

I remember once when our 7-year-old son made a last-second basketball shot that tied the game. I sat there, with everyone else, in complete anticipation, waiting for the ball to go through the hoop. When it did, I was the first one on my feet cheering. I remember the first place he looked was in the stands to see if I was, indeed, cheering. He wanted my approval. And he got it.

I want my Father's approval as well. Guess what? It isn't that difficult to receive. In my experience, God rewards simple obedience, childlike faith, and committed love. God looks for humble servants who are willing to openly and honestly approach His throne of grace, whereupon they will find mercy and strength in their time of need.

The truth is, God's approval is based less on what we do and more on who we are in Christ. God is seeking those who will simply call Him *Lord* and want to spend time with Him. He wants to reward us as good and faithful servants. If you are His child, listen to the approval of your Heavenly Father today.

Prayer: Lord, thank You for basing your approval of me not on what I do, but on who I am in Christ and what He did for me.

Reflect: When was the last time you reflected on what God thinks about you? Spend a few minutes listening to His approval today.

9 Imitators of God

Therefore, be imitators of God, as dearly loved children.

—EPHESIANS 5:1 CSB

In the home where we raised our boys, my wife had her own bathroom. You know, it's the one where she kept all her "stuff." I didn't even know what some of that stuff was. My two boys and I were allowed in there only in the strictest emergency situations, as long as we didn't leave a mess and didn't bother any of the stuff (I'm only slightly joking).

On a shelf in her bathroom, my wife's name was spelled out in individual block letters that were a Christmas gift from our oldest son.

It is well-known in my family that I like to tease my wife. It is one of the ways I show her I love her (I hope she knows that). One day, I began a repetitive practice of rearranging the letters in my wife's name. It was amazing how many words you can spell with just six letters (you may not be able to find some of them in the dictionary, but they worked for me). I'm sure it wasn't funny to anyone else at the time, but it was to me.

One day, while spelling a new word with the letters, my youngest son came into the room. "What are you doing, Daddy?" he asked. As I explained to him, he burst out laughing. He thought it was the funniest thing he had ever seen. From that day on, he assumed full responsibility for switching the letters around to spell a new word.

Now, my point is that my sons were always watching. At 11 and eight years of age at the time, they were often imitators of my actions. It was scary at times to see how they would even think like me.

In the same way, you and I are to be imitators of God. By devoting ourselves to the study of His Word and developing our personal relationship with Him, we are to cultivate the "habits" of God. In all that we do, say, or even think, God needs to be our guide.

Let's strive to be an imitation of our Father today.

Prayer: Lord, help others see You in me today. Help me imitate You in all that I do.

Reflect: Think for a moment about ways your life does not reflect the ways of God. How could you be a better witness of God to the world?

10 Hearing from God

"I am the good Shepherd; I know my sheep and my sheep know me."

—JOHN 10:14 NIV

I am often asked, "How do I hear a word from God?" Great question. I think most Christians would strive to obey God, even into a difficult calling, if they only knew for sure they were hearing from Him.

We are not meant to wander aimlessly. God does not intend for us to live our lives without knowledge of His plan. He may make us wait to see the whole picture, but He wants us to hear His voice.

Here are a few tips to help you hear from God in your journey.

1. **Get to know Him.** That is the key to any relationship. How can you hear from God if you have never met Him? You can't meet Him apart from knowing His Son, Jesus. Once He is your Savior, the more time you spend with Him, the stronger your relationship with Him will be.

2. **Listen.** I know that sounds simple, but unless you are spending time trying to hear from God, it will never happen.

3. **Learn His voice.** When you first meet someone, it usually takes a few tries before you begin to recognize their voice over the telephone. If my mom calls, she doesn't have to say, "Ron, this is your mother." I know her voice

by now (it's when she says "Ronald" that I know I'm in trouble).

4. Check it with Scripture. If you have any doubt about what God is telling you, compare it to His Word. God will never contradict Himself. If you ever think God is telling you to cheat on your wife, you'd better start reading the Book.

5. Obey. If God speaks to you clearly, without question, and you know it complements what has already been written in His Word, don't waste another second before obeying. If you want your relationship to grow, you need to establish early on that you will follow His will for your life.

6. Enjoy. Hearing from God is a great thing. It doesn't even matter as much what He says. God called me into vocational ministry with only two words: "Trust Me!" The great miracle is that the Holy, powerful, and mighty God, the Creator, has spoken. That is an event.

Prayer: Lord, if You should choose to speak to me today, I am open to hearing from You.

Reflect: Have you ever heard from God? Think about the last time you felt God impressing something upon your heart. You may never hear from God audibly; I haven't, but most likely God has spoken—or is trying to speak. Listen.

11 Giving God All My Love

"Two people owed money to a certain moneylender. One owed him five hundred denarii, and the other fifty. Neither of them had the money to pay him back, so he canceled the debts of both. Now which of them will love him more?"

—LUKE 7:41-42 NIV

When Jesus asked this question of Simon the Pharisee, Simon answered Him and said that it was the one who had the bigger debt canceled that loved the moneylender more. If he had been on *Jeopardy!*, he would have been right because that was exactly the answer Jesus wanted.

I don't know your story, but, personally, I feel like the man who had the bigger debt canceled. My sin debt was great, and yet Jesus paid it all. Just the thought of His grace overwhelms me at times.

A friend of mine has an incredible testimony. It's really pretty horrible if you think about it. He was simply awful, a real scumbag (I am being facetious). One time, when he was in the eighth grade—now, wait a minute, are you sure you're ready for this?—*he skipped church choir practice one night*. True story.

Seriously, we were in an accountability meeting confessing our "biggest sins" to one another. That was his story. Can you believe it? And God's going to let *him* into Heaven! Wow! There's still hope for me.

I wish that was my testimony. I sometimes wish I could hide some of my painful past or mistakes I've made. I've even wished I could do as God does, forgive myself, and then forget that it ever happened.

Some of my past just ain't pretty. I have sinned and continue to sin. Sometimes, I get caught in the trap of Satan's temptations and find myself in a mess of trouble.

But let me tell you that when I consider how much God has done for me, how far He had to come to rescue me—when I recognize how great His grace is in my life—I can't help but assign Him all my love.

God has been so good to me, what else can I give Him but all my love?

Prayer: Lord, thank You for all the forgiveness You have extended to me. You deserve all my love and devotion in return.

Reflect: Think for a moment about the "biggest sins" you have ever committed. Don't dwell on them. Rather, reflect on them for a moment to remember the grace God has extended to you. Then, rejoice in His love for you.

12　Freed from People-Pleasing

Am I now trying to win the approval of human beings, or of God? Or am I trying to please people? If I were still trying to please people, I would not be a servant of Christ.

—GALATIANS 1:10 NIV

When I first became a pastor, I fell into a dangerous trap. I started caring too much about what people thought about me. Of course, I needed to conduct myself in a worthy manner. It was important that, as the Scripture commands, I be "above reproach" (1 Timothy 3:2 NIV). But it was more than that. I was often refusing to do what God would have me do because I wanted to keep wearing my figurative "favorite pastor" button.

It was through this season that I realized I had probably struggled with people-pleasing all my life. It impacted the clothes I wore, the car I drove, and the size of my house. Much of my life as a business owner and community-driven citizen were directed by my desire to protect my public image.

Yet, God wanted my complete obedience, regardless of how it might look or please other people. Over the next few years, I began to evaluate my decisions by considering a new standard. Before I made major decisions, I began to ask myself, "Am I doing this to satisfy other people or to affect how they see me?" Or, "Am I doing this because I know it is something God would have me do?"

In the process, two things happened. First, I started to make better decisions. Questions are a great evaluation tool. They force you to consider other aspects of the outcome and why you are doing what you are doing.

Second, and most helpful, I felt less pressure in my life from what others might think or say about me. It was not that I didn't care anymore. I was released from the pressure of trying to please other people. When I am being obedient and bringing pleasure to God with my decisions, I don't have to worry about what others think or say. It is truly a freeing way to live.

Prayer: Lord, help me live for Your approval.
Reflect: Where in your life are you trying so hard to please others that it is causing you stress or keeping you from obedience to God?

13 The Size of God

"Heaven is my throne, and the earth is my footstool. What kind of house will you build for me?" says the Lord.

—ACTS 7:49 NIV

I don't know everything about Heaven, but I am pretty sure about one thing: Heaven is apparently *big*.

Think about it this way. God says that Heaven is His throne. Notice that He didn't say it was His whole house. Heaven is apparently just where He sits to rule. And then, He says the earth is His footstool. Wow! Now, that will make you think.

Imagine that earth is simply a footstool. If I remember correctly, the earth is a mass nearly 25,000 miles in circumference. That's big. The United States represents about 6 percent of the land mass of the world, and yet it has almost 4 million square miles of dry land. I have driven 1,000 miles in one day, and it wore me out. Can you imagine driving cross-country? What about traveling around the world? Have you ever been on a 12- or 13-hour international flight? This earth seems big to me.

But to God, the earth is only a footstool.

Then, we consider Heaven. All the angels, perhaps thousands upon tens of thousands of angels. The mansions for all the saints and the streets of gold. God basically says, when talking about Heaven, "You ain't seen nothing yet."

And, yet, Heaven is only His throne.

The simple point I am trying to make is that God is big. God is an awesome and wondrous God. He is larger than our human minds can conceive. Stretch your mind a million times, and you and I will never get a handle on the size of our Creator God.

But that is not really the point of this devotional. As wonderful as it is to think about how large our God is, the point I want to make is even more personal than that. Even though God is bigger than we can imagine, He genuinely cares for you and me. The God who paints sunsets and shapes mountains knows your name. He even numbers the hairs on your head.

Now, ponder that thought throughout your day.

Prayer: God, forgive me for the times I've seen You as too small. Help me remember the vastness of You and Your glory.

Reflect: Take a few minutes to observe the works of God. Look for the big and the small. Try to see God's glory in His creation.

14 | Be a Shepherd

**Be shepherds of God's flock that is under your care,
watching over them—not because you must, but
because you are willing, as God wants you to be;
not pursuing dishonest gain, but eager to serve.**

—1 PETER 5:2 NIV

Years ago, when I owned an insurance agency, I went
through a season when it seemed like all my customers
needed something other than insurance. They would ask
me to pray for them. Several told me about issues in their
marriages. A couple even asked me where I attended
church. I had Christian plaques and sayings scattered
around my office, but it didn't occur to me that they were
serving as an invitation to engage me in deeper conver-
sation. It took me a while to realize that perhaps God was
allowing me to use my influence with my customers to
help them beyond their insurance needs.

What individuals have God placed in your path for
whom He intends you to be a shepherd? Have you ever
thought about that?

As we mature in our Christian life, God brings people to
us who need our influence. It might be to witness to them,
invite them to church, or to simply be a true friend to
them. It could be neighbors who have difficult family relationships. There could be coworkers who need prayer and
wise counsel. Sometimes, God will use us for extended

family situations and, of course, in our own immediate family.

The Body of Christ, also known as the church, is often God's vessel of caring to the world around us. It is easy to get distracted with meeting our own needs and desires. If your life is anything like mine, there never seems to be enough time just to do the things you have to do. But God has called us to be servants who care for the needs of others around us.

Notice how Peter also points out that not only do we serve others, but we are to do so willingly. There's an implication there of joy in service. We are not to serve because it is a command or because we want something in return. We are to serve simply because of who we are in Christ. We are shepherds of God's flock.

Prayer: Lord, help me today to be aware of those You would have me shepherd.
Reflect: Spend a couple of minutes and make a list of people God may be placing in your life so that you can care for them.

15 Trusting While You Wait

On that day a great persecution broke out against the church in Jerusalem, and all except the apostles were scattered throughout Judea and Samaria.

—ACTS 8:1 NIV

"Where are we going, daddy?"

"We're moving to Samaria."

"Samaria? But, daddy, that's so far from home. We don't know anyone in Samaria."

"We have to go, darling. It is not safe for us here."

"Oh, daddy, but the Samaritans are not like us."

"It will be all right! God will take care of us, wherever we go."

I can imagine the family discussions in first-century Christian homes when the church was being persecuted. In these times of a great spiritual awakening, the Christians were, more than ever, under pressure to be quiet about their faith. Running for their own safety, they must have wondered why this was happening to them. After all, hadn't they just received the Good News?

Don't misunderstand, God always knew what He was doing. It was all part of His plan. Keep in mind that it was Jesus who told the disciples to take the Gospel into Jerusalem, Judea, Samaria, and to the uttermost parts of the earth (Acts 1:8 NIV). How would the people hear of Jesus unless someone went? Can't you see it was all a part of the plan? Plus, Christ had told them they would suffer because of their relationship with Him.

God was not surprised by their dilemma. And God is not surprised by yours.

Struggling brother, to all of you who are in desperate situations right now, you may be wondering what God is up to. You may even question God's wisdom in your situation. Don't be moved. Stand firm in your faith. God, indeed, has a plan. Right now, wherever you are, if you are His child, then I guarantee that you are right in the middle of that plan.

In the case of today's verse, we only had to read seven chapters of Acts to figure out what God was doing. Hang tight and wait on Him to work His plan in your life.

Trust Him. He will get you there.

Prayer: God, I trust You. Even in the midst of uncertainty, I know You are in control. Help me remember that continually.

Reflect: Take a few moments to reflect on how good God has been to you in your life, even during uncertain times. Perhaps God will use you to remind someone else of His faithfulness.

16 Creation Groans

The creation waits in eager expectation for the children of God to be revealed.

—ROMANS 8:19 NIV

Not long ago, my wife and I took a walk through our neighborhood on a breezy fall Sunday afternoon. The weather was perfect. The temperature was warm enough that we didn't need jackets but cool enough to walk without getting too hot. We took our time and enjoyed each other and being outdoors. The sun was shining brightly on what started as a cloudy day.

I am not always the most observant person, but I couldn't help but notice God's creation in a new way on this walk. I'm sure it was just the romantic mood we were in, but there seemed to be an inexpressible joy bursting out of each ray of light. God appeared so evident all around us.

As we walked, Cheryl would point to a dogwood and marvel at its beauty. Then, I would see some beautiful flowers in full bloom and quickly change our attention. We both took notice of the beautiful azalea bushes scattered throughout the yards. I had never seen such pure-white flowers in all my life. They were nearly perfect. I thought to myself, "God, you certainly know what you're doing" (as if He needed my affirmation).

The last year we were living in Kentucky, I remember noticing how the autumn trees were full of colors. I even commented to my wife that the colors were more vibrant than I had ever seen. During our walk on that Sunday, I made the same observation. My wife agreed. Then, we asked ourselves if we had been missing something, or if the colors really were better, brighter, and more glorious than ever before.

Could it be—do you think it is possible—that creation is improving all the more because it knows the day of His return is soon at hand? The Bible says that creation is groaning in anticipation. What started as a perfect display of His splendor was subject to decay at the fall of man. Now, as we near His second coming, perhaps creation is making itself more fully known, anxious to see Jesus return to this earth.

I don't know—it's just a suspicion on my part—but based on the creation I saw on our afternoon walk, He is coming soon.

Praise God, may it be true.

Prayer: Lord, thank You for the beauty of Your creation all around me.
Reflect: Take a few extra moments today, perhaps with a friend or loved one, and notice the wonder of God in His creation. Watch an ant methodically do its work. Notice the colors in a sunset. Ponder the majesty God displays in a cloud.

17 God Wants Me

> "And he is not served by human hands, as if he needed anything. Rather, he himself gives everyone life and breath and everything else."

> —ACTS 17:25 NIV

Sometimes, as I'm preparing a Bible study lesson, sermon, or writing a devotional, I have to be reminded that it is by God's strength that I am able. Like any pastor, I always appreciate when someone tells me they got something out of my message, but I try to always remember that God really could do it without me. In fact, there is likely nothing I do for God that someone else couldn't do better, if called by Him.

One of the joys of the Christian life is serving Christ, and I think He loves our service. But if we think about it, does God really need what we do for Him? After all, don't we serve the Creator God? Didn't He speak the heavens into existence? Isn't it He who decides when the rain will fall? Doesn't He tell the sun when it is time to shine, decorate the skies with the stars, hold the planets in position, and paint the rainbow when it appears?

Wasn't it God who told the eagle where to build its nest? Didn't He dictate the color of a zebra's stripes and determine how long a giraffe's neck would be? And wasn't it His decision to allow flies and gnats to remain after the fall?

I don't know about you, but I get the distinct impression that God knows what He is doing. What does He need from me? *Nothing.*

And yet, the reality that's even greater than that, even greater than getting to serve God, is that what He seems to want more than anything is to spend time with me. He doesn't need me, but He wants me. Like any good father, the Lord loves to spend time with His children. In fact, He wants me to spend my forever with Him in His Heavenly Home. He has invited me to take up a permanent residence among His chosen few. I'm going to the final wedding banquet. My name is written in the Book of Life.

God has all the wealth, power, and prestige of the world, and yet He chose to spend eternity with me. How cool is that? I can give Him nothing in return, but He accepts me anyway. By believing in Him, and by nothing else, I receive all the blessings of being His child.

I must tell you: That makes me feel pretty important.

Prayer: Lord, thank You for wanting to spend time with me and for preparing an eternity for us to be together.
Reflect: Spend a few moments reflecting on someday actually being in Heaven and eternally in the presence of God. Try to imagine the joy of being with Him and all the saints.

18 Surely Not I

They were very sad and began to say to him one after the other, "Surely you don't mean me, Lord?"

—MATTHEW 26:22 NIV

A number of years ago, as I was preparing to teach my Sunday school lesson to our young married class, the Lord began to impress on my heart that a couple in our class was having serious marital problems. It was such a strong impression that I asked the class to commit to pray for each other and their families.

A few short weeks later, I found out who the couple was. They came to me, and we were able to get them some counseling. Praise God, that couple is still together and appears to be doing very well at the time of this writing.

I must tell you, however, that this couple was the very last I would have ever guessed was having problems. Yet it shouldn't have surprised me, either.

Sometimes, those of us who call ourselves faithful Christians think that we can't possibly fall into that level of temptation; but men, Satan is busy. He knows his days are numbered. He wants to take away from the numbers being added to the church of God. He wants to destroy homes through lies and deception. He wants to infiltrate the lives of your children, distracting them from truth and leading them astray. He wants you to miss out on your time with God each morning. He wants to ruin your personal life and your marriage.

Christian men, we must stand strong. We must be on our guard and keep ourselves grounded in the Word of God. We must not give the Devil a foothold.

Get close to God. Hang on to Him tighter every day. Greater is He that is in us than he that is in the world. The Devil has no hold on us when we are holding onto Jesus.

Then, we can say with assurance, "Surely not I!"

Prayer: Lord, keep me close to You today. Protect me from temptation and guard my heart.
Reflect: Think for a moment about areas of your life where you are facing the greatest temptation. Confess to the Lord and maybe someone you trust. Get help before it is too late.

19 Following the Example of Jesus

After Jesus had finished instructing his twelve disciples, he went on from there to teach and preach in the towns of Galilee.

—MATTHEW 11:1 NIV

I get two very important messages from today's verse.

First, it is vital that we instruct our own disciples. If you are a father, you play a crucial role in the development of your children's spiritual lives. Ultimately, it is not up to the local church or your pastor to teach your children about Jesus. Don't misunderstand, they are valuable in the process. Your children need to be in the church regularly, in my opinion, but the primary mission is your responsibility.

God has given the task of discipling children to the parents. If your children know you are active in the church or other work but they never hear you tell them about Christ, they will lose the significance of the work. Teach them first.

Your children need your spiritual influence. They need to see you trusting your Heavenly Father. They need to hear you pray and watch you give and serve. They will be witnessing your commitment to Christ. Jesus took the discipling of His circle of followers very seriously, and it was in their lives that He first invested Himself. We need to follow His example.

Second, after Jesus instructed His disciples, He went out into the world to spread the Good News. There are some movements among Christians these days to separate themselves completely from the outside world. I can tell you that, in part, I agree. If the choice were all mine, my only associations would sometimes be just my Christian friends. It is with them that I find the most comfort and strength.

God, however, has called us to be in the world, but not of the world. How will we reach a lost world for Christ unless we are going to the unsaved? After we have invested in the lives of our family, it is our responsibility to be involved in the missions of the church. We must find a place of service where we can obey God's great commission.

If we want to be like Jesus, we will start at home, and then reach out to the world around us.

Prayer: Lord, make me more aware of my role as a disciple-maker in my own home and in the world around me.
Reflect: Spend a few minutes thinking of ways you can better share about your relationship with Christ to your family and to those who may not yet know Him.

20 Jesus in the Boat of Life

Suddenly a furious storm came up on the lake, so that the waves swept over the boat. But Jesus was sleeping.

—MATTHEW 8:24 NIV

A number of years ago, when our boys were still living at home, my family took a trip to the beach. Beach vacations were a great time of relaxation and reflection. Some of the best times for us as a family were when we were away from our everyday surroundings.

One morning, my eight-year-old son, Nathaniel, and I let the rest of the family sleep in while we went for a walk on the beach. That day, God used my son to remind me of a powerful truth.

It was midmorning on the beach. Surrounding us were dark clouds forming in the sky. It looked as if it could rain at any time. Suddenly, there were loud claps of thunder and lightning in the distance. I could tell it was still a safe distance away, but we started heading back to our room as a precaution.

About half a mile out to sea, there was a small sailboat. We had been watching the boat for several minutes. The captain seemed to be straining to get the vessel back on course, obviously to avoid the storm.

I commented to my son, "I sure wouldn't want to be on that boat when the storm came." Without any cue from me, my son replied, "Not unless Jesus was asleep in it."

Amen. That's right, son. Not unless Jesus was aboard.

It was a strong reminder. I don't want to be on any boat in my life or go through any storm unless Jesus is right in the middle. I want Jesus in the boat of my work life. I want Jesus in the middle of my marriage, my family life, and even my thoughts. If there is any boat in my life, my only hope, when the storms of life come, is that Jesus is in the boat with me.

Take a good reminder from my son. Don't sail on the boat of life without Jesus.

Prayer: Lord, help me keep You in the center of my life. Guard me from the storms of life as I trust in You.

Reflect: Think about aspects of your life for a moment. Is there any "boat" of your life from which Jesus is missing?

21 No More of This!

But Jesus answered, "No more of this!" And he touched the man's ear and healed him.

—LUKE 22:51 NIV

What else would we expect from Peter? He was the disciple most likely to act on impulse, right? Once, in the middle of a lake, Peter jumped out of the boat and tried to greet Jesus, who was walking on the water. Peter was quick to volunteer to build a tent for Jesus, Moses, and Elijah on the Mount of Transfiguration. Peter quickly dropped his successful fishing career to follow Jesus. Peter acted quickly when he was intent on a subject.

In this verse from Scripture, his Savior is confronted by a mob of soldiers. Peter couldn't believe their audacity. This was Jesus, the Son of God, who had come to save His people from their sins. Here is the miracle worker; even the winds and the waves obey Him. What could they mean by confronting Him in this way?

Even when he was outnumbered, Peter would fight for Jesus. Of course, Peter was acting on impulse. How dare anyone challenge his Lord.

But Jesus had other plans. Just as quickly as He rebuked the wind on a storm-tossed boat, He halted any further attempt to stop His arrest. This was a part of the divine plan of the Master.

Jesus had come not to bring conflict but to offer peace. Jesus had come so that no more would men have to rely on their own human strength and abilities. Jesus had come so that even Peter, who would ultimately not be capable of defending himself, might be able to rest upon the Lord. Jesus had come to bring victory to His people. This was all happening within the Father's will.

Perhaps there is something in your life today, something too difficult for you to handle alone. Perhaps you need a word from Jesus today that says, "No more of this!" No more suffering alone, no more crying without His tender concern, and no more struggling to make it on your own.

Jesus has come to offer to me and you, today, the miracle and the gift of His life.

Prayer: Lord, help me trust You today with whatever comes my way. Speak truth into the chaos of my life.

Reflect: Think for a moment about one area of your life where you would most welcome the hand of God upon you. Where would you most like Jesus to say, "No more of this"?

The Jesus Formula

Jesus then took the loaves, gave thanks, and distributed to those who were seated as much as they wanted. He did the same with the fish.

—JOHN 6:11 NIV

I wonder what the formula was. Have you ever thought about that when you've read this story? What was the formula Jesus used?

If you recall, Jesus had asked the disciples how many loaves they had. They surveyed the crowd and found a boy who had five loaves of bread and two fish.

So, what was the formula?

With that information, Jesus must have based his calculation on the number of people, and then carefully, mathematically, and meticulously divided the loaves and fishes so that everyone could eat until they were full and have exactly 12 baskets filled with leftovers (one for each disciple). What was the formula? Did it involve calculus or algebra?

I can almost hear Jesus now, talking to the disciples and wiping the sweat from His brow, "Whew, glad there weren't 400 more people, guys. We would have never fed them." This complicated separation and multiplication procedure was obviously invented by a higher mind than most mathematicians I know.

Of course, I am being somewhat facetious, but I'm trying to illustrate a point.

Jesus didn't need math. Jesus used the power given to Him by His Father, Almighty God. Jesus spoke it into existence as all of creation was formed. And when Jesus spoke, the people were fed. Jesus, by faith, told the people to sit down, and what started as a small snack for a little boy became a huge banquet for nearly 10,000 people. Jesus didn't need a formula. He *is* the formula.

Do you have anything in your life for which a little of Jesus could go a long way? Jesus is waiting to apply His miracles to your life when we, the children of God, co-heirs with Jesus to the throne, will humbly seek Him and give Him priority in our lives.

What is the formula for the answer to your struggles today? My friends, make no mistake about it. Whatever problem you have, the answer is Jesus!

Prayer: Lord, remind me today and throughout the day that You are the answer to all my needs.

Reflect: Think for a moment about what you currently have in front of you and in the days ahead. Where do you most need a miracle of Jesus?

23 Manly Meekness

Blessed are the meek, for they will inherit the earth.

—MATTHEW 5:5 NIV

We have a hard time with that verse sometimes, don't we?

Meekness 101 is not a popular course in our universities or even in our churches, and it's certainly not usually the topic of discussion at a wild-game dinner or men's retreat. We would much rather talk about the most popular ways to get ahead or how to fight like a warrior than how to discover riches through meekness.

This writer won't pretend to be an expert on the subject either, but I also won't ignore the Word of God. Blessed are the meek, for they shall inherit the earth.

Merriam-Webster defines *meek* as "enduring injury with patience and without resentment." I don't think Merriam-Webster is far off from the meaning intended in Scripture. The same is true of Merriam-Webster's definition of *meekness*: "a mild, moderate, humble, or submissive quality."

Wow, easily imposed upon, submissive; are those the qualities you and I want to teach our children?

But when we understand this from God's perspective, we can be meek and still be manly.

John the Baptist said that he must decrease for Christ to increase in his life (John 3:30). I think that's the idea behind meekness. We put Christ first, others second, and ourselves third. Putting others' interests ahead of our own may not appeal to our intellect, schooling, or "keen business sense," but it relates to a heart that loves God and desires the things He desires.

Meekness will require us to accept instruction and counsel from Him and from others. It will force us to submit to authority and not explode when others dare challenge our position or role.

Meekness may not meet the textbook definition of how we demand success in life, but it will put us into the right relationship with God. We are in a bless-able position with the Creator and Sustainer of life. The reward for meekness is an eternal inheritance that will outweigh all this world has to offer.

Meekness may not include the retirement plan you have been working for, but it's one I encourage you to invest in fully today.

Prayer: Lord, help me today to demonstrate meekness to those around me.

Reflect: Spend a few minutes reflecting on the word, *meekness*. Considering it in light of John the Baptist's statement above. How much is your life defined by meekness?

24 Sitting Together in Heaven

I hope to see you soon, and we will talk face to face.
—3 JOHN 1:14 NIV

If you don't have anything to do for the next five minutes, how about dreaming out loud with me?

Who do you long to see in Heaven? Have you ever thought about that?

I have been so blessed with friends on earth, but I really wish I had more time to just sit around and visit. Do you agree? I'm looking forward to that part of Heaven.

My wife and boys will feel like I really do prioritize spending time with them. We'll play the games we never started and finish the discussions that got interrupted.

I will enjoy getting to know my brother again. It seems like so long ago that we shared a room. I'll have longer than a car ride between meetings to talk with my sister. I will have plenty of time for my parents.

I will sit down with both of my grandmothers and grandfathers and let them tell me what it was like when they were growing up.

Then, there's my new friend Ryan, and my old friend Ryan. My friends Chuck, Steve, Dennis, Keith, and Tommy.

I want to sit down with great men of the Bible, too. Paul, Abraham, Moses, David, Elijah, Isaiah, and Jeremiah are just a few that come to mind. I will listen to Noah's stories about the worst flood of his life and how Jonah counted the ribs of a fish from the inside. I will visit with John as we compare the revelation he saw of the actual Heaven.

But wait a minute! Some people are not going to be there, are they? I was about to continue my list, but it dawned on me. The Bible says that no man comes to the Father (Heaven) "except by me" (Jesus) (John 14:6). That could be (*will be*) a problem if someone has never received Jesus Christ as their personal Lord and Savior.

Help me out here! I really want to see you face-to-face someday in Heaven. It will mean a lot to me (not to mention what it will mean to you). If there has never been a time where you, by faith, asked Jesus to save you from your sins, then do so today. Don't wait another moment.

And whoever you know who you couldn't add to your list. Why not share Jesus with them today?

Prayer: Lord, keep Heaven in my mind today as I reflect on being with you and those I love.

Reflect: Spend a few moments and make a list of those you know you'll see in Heaven someday and those you aren't certain about.

25 Unconditional Love

Let us then approach God's throne of grace with confidence, so that we may receive mercy and find grace to help us in our time of need.

—HEBREWS 4:16 NIV

Unconditional love. Have you ever experienced this awesome feeling? Until I became a pastor, I never realized how many people struggle with understanding the concept of unconditional love.

I feel so blessed to have grown up with this kind of love. My mother loves her children no matter what. I honestly believe there is nothing I could do for which she would not find a way to support me. She may not always agree with me, and she may be quick to point that out, but I have always known that I have one person in my corner.

My mother surrounded her children with unconditional love. I know I disappointed my mother many times—as all kids do—while growing up. Disappointment never caused disapproval of me as a person, however. I was always my mother's son. Period. I am always welcome, supported continuously, and reaffirmed often.

I hope you had that experience because it will go a long way toward understanding the deep love of our wonderful God. The truth is, however, that no matter what our experience is, we cannot fathom the depth of God's love for His children (Ephesians 3:19 NLT).

God's love is deeper than our level of comprehension. He loves us, not because of who we are, but because of who *He* is. He is God. He made us in His image so that He could love us and we could love Him. He doesn't just give us love; He is love.

And I believe it's safe to say that, whether or not you are a child of God, God loves you unconditionally. You didn't earn it. You don't deserve it. You couldn't buy it and you can't sell it. His love is yours whether you accept it or not. You cannot stop His love based on your behavior.

I don't mean to oversimplify this, but I need to make sure I am clear on this one topic: *God loves you*. And He always will.

Thank you, mom, for loving me unconditionally! You must have learned it from our mutual Dad!

Prayer: Lord, thank You for Your unconditional love.
Reflect: Do you have someone who has modeled unconditional love to you? If they are still living, perhaps send them a note of thanks today. If not, perhaps you will be that model for someone in your life.

26 Love of Money

Keep your lives free from the love of money and be content with what you have, because God has said, "Never will I leave you; never will I forsake you."

—HEBREWS 13:5 NIV

Notice that God didn't say not to like money. He didn't say you don't need money. He didn't say you should not acquire money. He certainly didn't say He didn't have money. He said to keep yourselves free from the *love* of money.

God is doing us a favor here. You and I both know that money is a necessary evil in society. It is needed to provide for the basics of life. Food, clothing, and shelter must be paid for by someone. Money must be exchanged at some level.

God knows that. What God is saying to us here is that we should *free* ourselves by letting go of the *love* of money. This word, *love*, means placing your whole will and emotions into the practice of loving. In other words, you have chosen to love something, and you like it. You not only have chosen to love money, but you really enjoy your times of loving money. It gets you excited.

I might compare it to a love relationship with a spouse. You have chosen, because of your legal commitment, to love this person (through good times and bad). There are certain times, however, when you really "feel" in love. You can't wait to be around them. You want to shower them with attention. You want to please them. That is the love based on emotion.

God wants us to be free of that type of love for money so that we can place our love in the proper perspective. We are to love Christ with all our heart, mind, and soul and love our neighbor as ourselves. When we give this kind of love to God, we are free from the burden of dependence on money. Instead, we can be totally dependent on God, who owns it all.

I need this encouragement as much as you do. We need to rid ourselves of the fascination with money and allow ourselves to be fascinated by the awesomeness of the Creator. It is then that we will begin to achieve real peace, contentment, freedom, and the glory of God.

Prayer: Lord, help me trust You completely, above every earthly possession.

Reflect: Think for a moment what impact money and the pursuit of it has on your life. Be willing to admit to yourself if any part of that is unhealthy.

27 Daddy's Shoulders

But you, God, see the trouble of the afflicted; you consider their grief and take it in hand. The victims commit themselves to you; you are the helper of the fatherless.

—PSALM 10:14 NIV

When my youngest son was three years old, he was very shy in public. A stranger would come up to take notice of the cute little blonde, and the more the person tried to get my son's attention, the more my son would hide his face. We called it shy, but it was really a son seeking protection from his father.

The person was just trying to be nice. The cute little boy cowered, however, into his daddy's shoulder.

Do you ever feel the need to seek your Heavenly Father's protection?

In life, as we grow older, we see so many hardships. We endure struggles and heartaches. We are sometimes tempted to say, "Where is God in all this?" We often fail to recognize God amid trials (He really is there all the time).

May I assure you of something today? Just as the Psalmist said, God does see trouble and grief. Our Father is not oblivious to our pain. He is carefully watching over His children. At just the right time, God will literally take our struggles in His mighty hand and lift us up out of our pit of despair.

The Psalmist talks about the victim. Have you ever felt like a victim? Do you often feel there is nowhere to turn? Are you a victim of this broken world?

Picture for a moment being a two-year-old who has lost his parents in a crowded mall. How do you feel? Do you sometimes have that feeling in the world today?

Praise God, He wants to protect His children. God is looking for victims who will call upon His name. God wants to comfort the fatherless in their distress.

Why not climb up into Daddy's lap today? I'm sure you are strong and have weathered much in this life, but why not rest your weary head on His powerful shoulder? Cast your burdens upon Him because He cares for you. Tell Him that cute little blonde boy sent you!

Prayer: God, thank You for caring for me like a Good Father.

Reflect: Think for a moment about the way God has and is caring for you. In what ways has He protected you from this world?

28 God Running

So he got up and went to his father. But while he was still a long way off, his father saw him and was filled with compassion for him; he ran to his son, threw his arms around him and kissed him.

—LUKE 15:20 NIV

One of the finest word pictures in the Bible is God running to His children.

Jesus told the parable of the lost son, foolish in his youth, who squanders away all his wealth, and then comes cowering back to his father, who surprises him by welcoming him with open arms.

Jesus used parables to teach principles, and in the Parable of the Prodigal Son, Jesus is describing for us how God feels about His children.

Stop for a moment and picture this story as Jesus meant for you to. You are the prodigal child. You have wandered away from the comfort and protection of your Father God. You have wasted your life on wild living. It was fun at first, but then the newness wore off and you got homesick. What you wouldn't give to go home.

But, how could you? You have traveled so far. Your pride is at stake. People would say, "I told you so." How could your Father ever forgive you for what you have done? And, does He really want you to come home, anyway?

Still, anything is better than where you are currently. So, you head for home. But before you can even see the front porch, while your head is still hanging low, you hear a sound. It sounds like footsteps. Heavy footsteps. You look up, almost afraid to, and you see a sight never seen before.

God is running to meet you. God, the Creator of stars, is running to greet you, a sinner, and welcome you home. He isn't coming with a frown or an angry smirk on His face. His arms are open wide. He has a great big smile. He has that loving twinkle in His eye, the kind He always had when He was proud of something you did.

He reaches you, and, instead of shouting insults at you, He tells you how pleased He is to have you home. He lets out a shout of joy. He orders a party to be held in your honor. *God is glad you have come home!*

Maybe you need to go home today. God is waiting. He's probably halfway toward you right now. All you have to do is turn around and head for home.

Prayer: God, thank You for the story of the Prodigal Son and for reminding me that You will run to greet me when I return home.

Reflect: Spend a moment reflecting on times you've veered from the path God has for you and the way it felt when you returned.

In Time You'll Understand

Jesus replied, "You do not realize now what I am doing, but later you will understand."

—JOHN 13:7 NIV

Obviously, Jesus wasn't talking to me when He said this some 2,000 years ago, but I can tell you that He has said it to me many times. In fact, in the years I have walked with Him, it is probably His most common comment to me, or at least it seems that way.

I often find myself questioning what God is up to in my life. I can be in the middle of experiencing a season of calm, and seemingly out of nowhere comes a major trial of life. I am tempted to say, "What is going on, God?" Have you ever felt that way?

I can be experiencing one of the terrific mountain-top journeys in life, and then I am hit with a tremendous obstacle, leaving me with no recourse but to pray.

I don't understand times like that.

And in reflection, I wonder if God is trying to teach me something. Do you think maybe He wants me to depend on Him in the good times and the bad? Do you think He wants to be the God of my mountains as well as my valleys?

The reality is that I have no problem asking, seeking, and knocking when times are bad in my life. No one has to convince me I need God when I'm stressed. I'm on my knees quicker than you can say, "Don't forget the knee-pads, man!"

But when times are good, I often feel strong enough on my own. I may settle into my routine of token prayers. I may fail to trust that God will meet my every need.

Sometimes, I believe trials come because Jesus wants to remind me that what I may not understand now, in time I will.

And you will, too.

Prayer: Lord, in the times I don't understand, help me trust that You have everything under control.
Reflect: What are some things you simply can't understand right now? What do you hope God will someday make clearer for you?

30 Heart and Soul

"Do all that you have in mind," his armor-bearer said. "Go ahead; I am with you heart and soul."

—1 SAMUEL 14:7 NIV

I want you to think for a moment about what isn't written in this verse. The armor-bearer was a servant to Jonathan. This servant didn't have to obey willingly, but he had to obey. It was his job to serve Jonathan, but he didn't have to *want* to obey. There is a difference. He was obliged by the fact that he worked for Jonathan to obey the command, but he didn't have to enjoy doing it. He didn't have to serve with his "heart and soul."

Jonathan had told his armor-bearer that he wanted to attack the enemy. It was one of those there-are-more-of-them-than-us situations. Jonathan was placing his faith in God and asking his servant to follow along. The armor-bearer—we don't even know his name—placed his faith in God through Jonathan. Now, that takes conviction!

Jonathan had seen God work. He knew the power of the Almighty. He had access to the great priests of the faith. He had position and authority.

The nameless armor-bearer most likely only knew what Jonathan had told him about God. Yet, he apparently saw something in Jonathan that told him it would be okay. So, he willingly committed his very life—heart and soul—to the cause.

Would anyone be willing to do that with us today? Do you and I have a faith in God that is so evident that, even if those watching us did not know God personally, they would follow Him based solely on our testimony?

These are sobering questions. Obviously, I hope my two sons would feel that way about me. I hope my wife would (although her faith appears stronger than mine most days). But imagine what it would be like if the people who work with us and for us were willing to walk by faith simply because they knew our character and the trust we have in God.

Prayer: Lord, help me live my life so that others would follow You because they would follow me.

Reflect: Think about the people in your life who need a witness of the character of God. Could you be that example for them?

31 Strength in Weakness

*I came to you in weakness with great fear
and trembling.*

—1 CORINTHIANS 2:3 NIV

God likes it when we come to Him in weakness. In fact,
in my experience with God, He is attracted to weakness.
Whenever I am at my lowest, God seems to be at His
best. That may sound strange unless you realize how
much God wants to help His children.

Years ago, through no fault of my own, I found myself
in a desperate financial situation. I was starting a business, and if you've ever been in business, you understand
the term, *cash flow*. This particular month, cash was
stretched. I was literally down to my last few dollars in my
checking account. I had an immediate need for $126.53 to
pay my electric and water bills. Being paid strictly on
commission, and then only once a month, I knew that in
the two weeks until payday my house would be without
utilities.

I prayed fervently before God. I needed a miracle, and
I needed one fast—by the 4 p.m. cut-off deadline, to be
exact. As I poured out my heart to God, I remembered I
had credit available on a credit card. I hurried to the bank
to get a cash advance, then rushed the money to the
utility companies. I praised God for giving me an "answer"
along the way.

I went home early, exhausted by the spiritual events of the day. I opened my mail and there was a life insurance refund check I never expected in the amount of $250. And I had 15 minutes to spare. God is never late and never early.

That day, I knew that God is who He claims to be. I knew that when He said He would provide that He *would* provide. I didn't have to depend on artificial resources.

God was ready to help me that day, not because of anything I had done for Him, but because of what He wanted to do for me. He was attracted to my weakness.

Do you have any weaknesses today? How could God use them as you trust in Him?

Prayer: Lord, thank You for being perfectly strong in my weaknesses.
Reflect: What is one area of your life in which you know you are out of your league? Reflect on how you will practice turning that struggle over to God this week.

32 I've Had Enough!

Elijah was afraid and ran for his life. When he came to Beersheba in Judah, he left his servant there, while he himself went a day's journey into the wilderness. He came to a broom bush, sat down under it and prayed that he might die. "I have had enough, LORD," he said. "Take my life; I am no better than my ancestors." Then he lay down under the bush and fell asleep.

—1 KINGS 19:3-5 NIV

The last prophet of the day was at his bitter end. This man, Elijah, sold out for service to the Creator God, was ready to give back his life. Have you ever felt like giving up on life?

Elijah had preached to the lost and been a great messenger of God's Word to the Israelites. He had witnessed numerous miracles in his personal life and in the lives of those around him. He had seen the dead raised and the poor provided for. Elijah saw hundreds of Israelites turn from their worship of Baal back to God. One of the greatest miracles of the Bible had occurred by God's power and with Elijah's faith and leadership. Elijah was at the prime of his ministry.

And yet, he was ready to die.

Jezebel, the wicked queen, had sent a message to Elijah that she intended to have him killed. Elijah was scared. He was terrified. After this spiritual high of seeing the Lord literally rain fire from the heavens, Elijah found himself in the middle of a mess.

Am I sadistic if I find comfort in that today? Not that I'm glad Elijah was distressed enough to want his life to end, but if this can happen to Elijah, then I shouldn't be surprised that it can happen to me. Doesn't it make you feel better that Elijah, a prophet of the Old Testament, who had personally been fed by the angels (that has never happened to me), could struggle through life at times? Don't you gain a little more peace in knowing that if Elijah isn't expected to be perfect, then maybe you and I don't have to be perfect either?

God didn't strike Elijah down. He lifted Elijah up and strengthened him for the next task. He encouraged Elijah.

Wherever you are today, whatever you are going through, God is working on your behalf. Just like Elijah, God will hear your prayer and strengthen you.

So, tell God when you have simply had enough. He will understand.

Prayer: Thank You, Lord, for when I am ready to give up, You still have a plan. Help me trust You more.
Reflect: Think about Elijah's dilemma for a moment. In what ways can you identify with him today?

33 Don't Talk, Listen

Know this, my beloved brothers: let every person be quick to hear, slow to speak, slow to anger; for the anger of man does not produce the righteousness of God.

—JAMES 1:19-20 ESV

On every personality profile, I assess as a take-charge individual. My top StrengthsFinder result is Command. I am an eight on the Enneagram. I have a High D on Disc, with no other letters even registering. If no one is leading, I will quickly step into the role. While this has served me well in my career and even as a pastor, I have also learned it is not always the holiest way to live.

As I have grown in my faith, God has challenged areas of my personality that are often outside of His ultimate desire for me. Sometimes, in my relationship with God, I need to be quiet and still. In my family relationships, I need to take time to be present and not try to be the one in charge or leading every discussion. In my leadership, I can be more effective if I listen more than I talk. I need to ask more questions than I answer. When things do not go as I would want them to go, displaying patience gains more favor with others than quickly showing my displeasure.

I am far from perfect in any of this. I continue to be a work in progress. My personality has not changed. I still have a tendency to take over a room if I do not consciously choose otherwise. But over the years, as I have tried to grow in these areas, I have become more effective in all my relationships. My time with God is more impactful. My family seems more valued and appreciated. The teams I lead are more productive. They sometimes lead without me, and we accomplish so much more than we could ever produce when I had to be at the center of control.

These examples are a reminder that God is not finished with me as a disciple. They also remind me that His ways are best and when I follow His commands, every relationship in my life is better.

Prayer: God, help me be quiet when I need to be today.
Reflect: How are your listening skills? Who in your life could benefit from you not having an answer and just sharing your presence?

Watch and Pray

"Watch and pray so that you will not fall into temptation. The spirit is willing, but the flesh is weak."

—MATTHEW 26:41 NIV

Jesus warned the disciples to watch and pray. There is such a huge word for us here.

Jesus was about to take the long and brutal walk to the Cross. He knew that the next few weeks for the disciples would be difficult. He had prepared them over several years of ministry, and now it was time for them to live up to their call.

Notice that Jesus didn't tell the disciples to simply "pray." He told them, instead, to "watch and pray."

Prayer is the lifeblood of every believer, but sometimes, I think we confuse prayer for its purpose. God certainly wants us to pray. In fact, He tells us to pray without ceasing and in all circumstances. We are to pray whether we have plenty or not enough.

But God did not tell us to pray, and then sit down on the job. No, as in this case, He says to "watch and pray." In other words, it is important to remember that while we wait on God, we are to keep on doing what we know to be right.

I was given an example of this once while talking with a man I had just met. He had been in town for over a year and still had not found a church home. He said he was waiting on God to reveal which church he should go to, and God just hadn't told him yet.

In fact, though, God really had. He says plainly in His Word that we are not to forsake the assembling of believers (Hebrews 10:24-25). So, if you aren't gathering with believers now, then you aren't listening to or obeying God. In this case, I think God might say "visit and pray" because the spirit is willing, but the body is weak.

If you are waiting to hear from God, keep waiting. God will answer in due time. While you wait, keep praying, but also do the work you know to be within His will.

Keep watching while you pray.

Prayer: Lord, while I'm waiting for You, I'll keep on praying, but give me the strength to do all I know to do.

Reflect: Where in your life are you waiting on God and praying? Is there something you ought to be doing while you wait?

35 Prison Longings

I eagerly expect and hope that I will in no way be ashamed, but will have sufficient courage so that now as always Christ will be exalted in my body, whether by life or by death.

—PHILIPPIANS 1:20 NIV

Paul was in prison. His hands and feet were likely shackled in ways that would cut into his skin and impede his circulation. He was being persecuted for his faith. His faith in Jesus was something he had obtained in the second half of his life.

Paul had given up so much to follow Christ. His material possessions, which were once many, now consisted only of the clothes on his back. Yet he had resolved to live his life for Jesus Christ's glory and to that end alone.

Was it always easy? No. Paul said he had to learn the secret of being content. Did he never want for anything? Of course, he surely had natural desires. He was human, and there were certainly earthly pleasures he missed.

Was it worth it? You bet. All of Heaven was waiting for the opportunity to reward him for his faithfulness. Imagine your own pleasure the day you meet Paul in Heaven.

You and I have been summoned to a higher calling. We have been requested to take on a deeper commitment. Christ has asked us to lay everything on the line for the sake of His name. We have been bought with a high price. Our mission, now, is to honor and please the Father by glorifying His Son.

It won't be easy, but we pray that He will give us "sufficient courage" to stand the test of time. Then, on that bright day when Jesus comes to take His people Home, you and I will stand with Paul and receive that honor bestowed upon those who faithfully stood with Jesus and hear these words: "Well done, good and faithful servant" (Matthew 25:23 NIV).

The older I get, the more I look forward to hearing the praise given to God's children for our sacrifices here on earth.

Prayer: Dear Lord, please give me sufficient courage to see through the days ahead.
Reflect: Reflect on meeting God face-to-face for the first time. How will you feel? What will be your first reaction? What will you ask Him?

36 A Fearless Warrior

Therefore we will not fear, though the earth give way and the mountains fall into the heart of the sea.

—PSALM 46:2 NIV

The Psalmist has given us a command that is easier said than done. "Have no fear" may be one of the most repeated commands in the Bible, but that doesn't make it easy. I realize that, as men, we often receive a stereotype of being fearless, taking risks, and living as warriors. But, if we are honest, those stereotypes aren't necessarily realities in the heart of most men I know.

I raised two boys, who are now amazing young men. Of course, parental roles greatly overlap. But I felt it was my role as a father to teach them to be strong. Their mother's role was to nurture them, and they needed both, but I felt the need to show them how to stand the test of time. I wanted them to be able to demonstrate courage in a world that is often difficult and scary. When one of the boys got hit with a ball but was clearly not hurt, I was the one who got to say, "Hang in there. You're okay."

I must be honest, however. For me, "standing tough" is often not easy. There have been some trials I have faced that, frankly, scared me to death.

And, to be even more transparent, there have been times I've had financial struggles, relationship tensions, and work pressures that have come close to giving me anxiety attacks as I wrestled through them.

In the end, to remain "courageous" and have no fear, I have learned I need to personally choose not to be afraid. It's an inner resolve that, instead of drowning in fear, I would rest in God's provision for me and His tender care to see me through the trial. It is more of an inner resolve of faith than some supernatural strength at being manly.

We must make a conscious decision to place all our trust in God. We must choose His promises, by faith, over our fears. We must depend upon what we cannot see to defend ourselves against the real, tangible dangers in the world today.

For me, it takes an intentional effort and determination to be a fearless warrior of a man.

Prayer: God, help me today to have amazing courage because I'm trusting completely in You.

Reflect: Take a moment and think through your own process of finding courage. How do you discipline yourself to trust God in times of stress or during a trial?

37 In Step with the Spirit

**Since we live by the Spirit, let us keep in step
with the Spirit.**

—GALATIANS 5:25 NIV

Years ago, my family and I spent a hot July day at a theme park. We had been there most of the day and had a really good time. The boys were tired, and as hot as it was, we were ready for a rest and the coolness of our car. As we walked toward the exit, we passed all the rides and attractions we had already seen. The walk back to the car seemed a lot longer than the walk into the park that morning. When we finally got to the exit, we realized that our car had been only yards away from where we started leaving the park. If only we had gone the other way, we would have avoided an almost 30-minute walk in the heat and humidity.

There have been countless times I have struggled through a situation only to realize that I should have done things differently. Most of those times, I should have trusted God or sought His guidance. Had I waited on His timing to be revealed rather than taking things into my own hands, the outcome may not have come quicker, but the journey would have been less painful.

God has provided a resource to us. Sadly, we don't take enough advantage of it.

As followers of Christ, we have a built-in guide to help us in life. God lives in us through His Spirit. We have a

Heavenly investment in us, which has been given to us as a hope and a promise of the eternal Home that is to come, but also as a partner to lead and guide us through every phase of life.

I'm convinced that the greatest struggle we have in the Christian life is to learn to walk in step with the Spirit of God. The gift of the Spirit to us is real, but our challenge is to accept the gift. That's what it means to "lean not on your own understanding" (Proverbs 3:5 NIV). It's what Jesus meant when He talked about the vine and the branches (John 15 NIV). He promised that if we remain in Him, we will bear much fruit.

Today, may we strive to walk in step with the Spirit.

Prayer: God, thank You for the gift of the Spirit. Help me walk in step with You today.

Reflect: Think about some decisions you've made that, when you look back at them now, you wish you could have done differently. Make a verbal commitment to learn from your experience.

38 Finding My Certain Place

One day Jesus was praying in a certain place.

—LUKE 11:1 NIV

I have visited the Holy Land and walked the paths and stood in places where Jesus likely walked and stood. One of the most moving places for me is the garden where Jesus prayed the night He was arrested. I can picture the anguish He felt as He asked the disciples to stay awake and labor with Him in prayer.

I don't know which place Luke is referring to in today's verse, but what stands out to me is that Jesus went to a "certain place" to pray. Luke seems very descriptive in his use of the phrase to explain the procedure of the prayer time of Jesus.

In Genesis 28:11, Jacob also met God in a "certain place."

My question is simply this: Do you and I have a "certain place" where we regularly meet with our Heavenly Father?

I went to a dictionary for the meaning of the word, *certain*: 1. Definite or fixed; 2. Sure to come or happen; 3. Established beyond doubt; 4. Capable of being relied upon; 5. Assumed to be known.

Do those definitions in any way adequately describe your prayer life? Is it definite or fixed? Is your prayer routine something that is sure to come or happen? Can you say that your prayer life is established beyond doubt? Is the time you spend on your knees capable of being relied upon? Is it assumed to be known that, at a certain time or place, you will meet with the Maker of your soul?

Are you convicted by those questions as much as I am? Brother, I don't know about you, but if I am going to grow into the image of Christ, I have work to do in establishing my certain place before God.

Someone once said prayer is not *part* of the work. Prayer *is* the work of a believer. I wonder if establishing our certain place is a key part of genuinely being a person of prayer.

Prayer: Lord, I want to become even more a person of prayer. Help me find a certain place.
Reflect: Take a few moments and consider your own prayer life. Is it what you want it to be? What changes could you make to improve your prayer life?

39 Bubbles Vanish

All people are like grass, and all their glory is like the flowers of the field; the grass withers and the flowers fall, but the word of the Lord endures forever.

—1 PETER 1:24-25 NIV

Grass withers. Flowers fall. Trees decay and rocks crumble. And bubbles vanish.

Once, while on vacation, my boys and I spent many hours in the swimming pool of the cottage complex where we were staying. I don't know if you've been in a swimming pool lately with eight- and 10-year-old boys, but if not, let me tell you something. Boys like to run their hands swiftly across the water and thrust excess water into the air, slinging it on those who happen to be nearby. In other words, *boys splash*.

After one particular splash, one of the boys commented on the number of bubbles being created. Before we could examine his find, however, most of the bubbles had popped. To the boys, it was as if we had made a secret discovery: Bubbles vanish. Almost as quickly as the bubbles were created, they disappeared. We tested it several times.

Now, more than 20 years later, I'm testing this discovery all over again with my young granddaughter. Bubbles can be so much fun.

The bubble discovery was a terrific teaching moment with my boys (if you are raising children, always look for teaching moments). In that moment in the swimming pool with my boys, I was reminded that, just like the bubbles, we too, quickly vanish from this earth. I was able to point out to my boys that day that whether we live to be 10 or 100, the life span of man is very short when compared to the age of mankind. Our lives are but a vapor. And that's why every second of our lives matters.

Plus, that truth makes our mission as Christians to gather disciples even more urgent. We must seize opportunities daily to share the Good News of Jesus Christ.

There is no time to waste in this life of ours. Bubbles vanish—and so do our opportunities to live for Christ.

Prayer: Lord, realizing how quickly life passes, help me make the best use of my days.
Reflect: Take a minute to reflect on your current calendar. Is your schedule aligned appropriately with what you value most in life?

40 Let the Little Children Come

Jesus said: "And whoever welcomes one such child in my name welcomes me."

—MATTHEW 18:5 NIV

We raised our boys in a military town. Though I was not in the military, many of our friends were. We went to church with literally hundreds of military families.

We often had young military families in the Bible study classes I taught. Most of them didn't have children yet or had very young children. Our boys were in elementary school, so it was common for them to enjoy the company of these military families. They were "cooler" than Cheryl and me.

One young soldier took a special interest in the boys. I learned a lot by watching how this young man interacted with my two sons. This strong, military trained, athletic leader had a special way of entertaining children. My boys loved him. They saw something in him that inspired them to want to be around him.

I welcomed it because he was such a good role model for them.

I love my boys and miss them being at home, but, quite honestly, sometimes I could lose my patience with them. They were so needy at times. They required so much attention. They asked so many questions.

My military friend had a warmth about him that my boys loved and made him fun to be around. Around him, my boys seemed to appreciate the smallest things in life.

They wrestled, played ball, and laughed. They didn't seem as affected by the worries of the world. They were simply kids.

Those interactions made me wonder if that was what Jesus was like. We know children seemed to want to be around Him. In fact, Jesus said, if we want to welcome Him, we must welcome the little child.

Shouldn't we strive to live our lives in such a way?

Of course, my friend was only with them for snippets of time, but the reality is that the pressures and strife of our world sometimes steal the joy we have for life. My friend not only made my children's lives better, he improved mine, too. He challenged me to help my kids be kids.

Prayer: Lord, help me live in such a way that welcomes the little children to come to me in joy.

Reflect: I have grandchildren now, and it's easy to find joy with them. If you have children in the home, think about the quality of your time with them. Does the atmosphere of your home welcome joy?

41 Learning from the Ants

My zeal wears me out, for my enemies ignore your words.

—PSALM 119:139 NIV

The Psalmist who wrote today's verse (most believe it was David) was excited about God. In fact, he was so excited that he wore himself out with service. Can you imagine what it would be like to have that level of faithfulness?

I once spent a season marveling over ants.

Every morning, I would sit on my back patio, drink my coffee, and read my Bible. For weeks, I was captivated by a trail of ants that began on one side of my patio and ended on the other side. It was about 20 feet long. The ants marched in a straight line, two ants going one direction, two going the opposite direction. They were spaced no more than an ant's distance apart from one another. There were hundreds of ants on my patio at any given time.

Now, when I first discovered there were ants on my patio each morning, I was not very excited. I tried spraying them with an ant killer. I tried washing them away with the garden hose. I tried stomping on them. I even got creative by trying to place obstacles in their way. I was actually starting to have fun with this project.

My attempt to rid the patio of ants went on for a week. They would disappear for a time. I was very good at getting rid of them temporarily. I felt successful every time I tried, but before I knew it, the line of ants was back again. And it seemed they came back bigger, stronger, and more determined than ever. I finally decided I liked these ants. They became *my* ants.

But watching the ants gave me an illustration for life. As I have watched the life of an ant, it occurred to me that just as they are diligent in their labor, so too should I be in mine. Those ants were doing exactly what they had been created to do. I am called to serve God as much as the Psalmist was, and I should be as diligent in seeking the Lord as He is in seeking after me.

My ants taught me a lot about determination and commitment. Praise God, I'm still teachable.

Prayer: Lord, help me have the commitment and diligence of an ant today!

Reflect: Think about your diligence in seeking God these days. Do you need to recommit your purpose and passion for Christ?

42 Meeting God in Unexpected Places

When Jesus saw Nathanael approaching, he said of him, "Here truly is an Israelite in whom there is no deceit."

I have been to Nazareth, and although it is much more modern and larger than it was in the days of Jesus, it isn't a place one would likely go to without a reason. Obviously, I went because Jesus had been there. Without that knowledge, I would have spent more time in Jerusalem or at the Sea of Galilee.

Nathanael was shocked. The Messiah had come from a small, relatively unknown city called Nazareth. He wondered if anything good could come from there. In Jesus's day, Nazareth wasn't known as a town of heroes. It was not a place where one might expect to see a world leader arise. The education system didn't produce the greatest students. It simply wasn't, in Nathanael's mind, the home of champions.

Nathanael, also called Bartholomew, was a man who spoke his mind. I don't think he was opposed to Christ coming from Nazareth. His view of God, however, just wouldn't allow such a thing to occur. He saw the Messiah as coming from the aristocratic neighborhoods of society. He thought the Messiah would display great wealth and strength. That simply didn't describe someone from Nazareth.

But, as we know the story, when Nathanael saw Christ, even though He was from Nazareth, he placed his whole faith and devotion in the Savior who had come from the forsaken town. Nathanael recognized that Jesus was the Son of the Living God. There was nothing false about his wholehearted devotion.

Perhaps we should be more like Nathanael. Maybe we should look for God in unexpected places. Quite possibly, God wants to surprise us by showing up at those awkward times of life. Perhaps God's glory will be found in the mundane moments and with people we might overlook.

I wonder if our view of God is too small sometimes. Are we ready, like Nathanael, to recognize Christ, the Son of the Living God, with all our heart?

Look for God, today, to show up when and where you least expect Him.

Prayer: God, help me look for You today in places and in ways I may have never imagined.

Reflect: Put Nathanael's perception into your context today. What city or country would it surprise you to learn that Jesus had come from?

43 Doubting Thomas

So the other disciples told [Thomas], "We have seen the Lord!" But he said to them, "Unless I see the nail marks in his hands and put my finger where the nails were, and put my hand into his side, I will not believe."

—JOHN 20:25 NIV

You have likely heard the term, "Doubting Thomas." We often use it to describe those who just can't quite believe something. They may want to believe, but there is still some skepticism that keeps them from accepting with full confidence.

The rest of the disciples had seen Jesus after his resurrection. Thomas had not been there. Perhaps he was still discouraged. His Savior—the One to whom he had devoted his life, the One he had trusted for safety—had been nailed to a tree. No more would he enjoy the companionship of the Son of Man. Perhaps he just couldn't convince himself to join the other disciples.

By not being there, however, he missed seeing Jesus. So, in order to believe the disciples, he wanted tangible proof. He wanted to see Jesus personally.

We tend to know Thomas best for his doubts, but he was also capable of displaying great courage. Some accounts of Thomas indicate that he became a great missionary in India during the first century. We do know that when Lazarus died and the disciples and Jesus went to be with him, Thomas said, "Let us also go, that we may die with him" (John 11:16 NIV).

Maybe it's not so bad to have doubts. Christ certainly didn't condemn Thomas. Appearing again to the disciples, Jesus allowed Thomas to see and feel that He was, indeed, the Risen Lord. Jesus accepted Thomas even with his doubts.

You and I, in the face of a sometimes dark world, will certainly have periods of doubt. We may experience times when our faith seems weak. Jesus, the Maker of our souls, would say to us as He said to Thomas: "Peace be with you. Stop doubting and believe."

And may we respond as Thomas did: "My Lord and my God!" (John 20:27-28).

Prayer: Lord, thank You for accepting me, doubts and all.
Reflect: Confess some of your current doubts or even questions you have in life these days. Then, reflect how God's truth can answer every doubt and question you have.

44 Mountain-Moving Faith

We live by faith, not by sight.

—2 CORINTHIANS 5:7 NIV

The world lives by sight, doesn't it? "Show me a pretty face, and I'll show you a million bucks." "Show me the money." "Either put up or shut up." "Show me what you're made of." "Let me see for myself."

Ever heard comments like that? Isn't that our society? If you can't prove it, then it isn't real.

And some of that is simply human nature. God made us a questioning species. He gave us the ability to think, reason, and create. I'm personally glad He did. Life would be boring without that ability.

In God's Kingdom, however, faith is an essential part of what we believe. In fact, seeing the outcome is really the opposite of faith. Faith is believing and being sure of something without the benefit of seeing it first. It is kind of like knowing, before your child is born, that you will love your child. That takes faith. If you could see it, then it wouldn't be faith.

We do not place Christian faith in something we can hold in our hands or see with our eyes. For instance, a person might have confidence in their bank accounts or job, but faith is much different than that. Faith is in a *person*. Faith is in the person of God. Faith is believing that God is who He claims to be and that God will do what He has promised to do.

Perhaps you need to renew your faith today. Perhaps you can't *see* how God will bring you through the current trials in your life. It doesn't make sense to trust in something (really some*one*) you can't touch or feel. And your emotions will often work against you in this. But, then again, that is what faith is all about: trusting blindly and without reservation in God's providence over your life.

I have some good news for you today. Jesus said that with faith the size of a mustard seed you can move mountains (Matthew 17:20 NIV).

Do you have any mountains (obstacles) in your way these days?

Prayer: God, help me trust You even when I cannot see the path forward.
Reflect: When was the last time God asked you to trust Him without all the answers? I encourage you to journal through those seasons. You'll need to look back and see how God delivered you every time.

Peter Had a Mother-in-Law

When Jesus came into Peter's house, he saw Peter's mother-in-law lying in bed with a fever.

—MATTHEW 8:14 NIV

This may seem like an obscure verse, but I think there is something to be learned here (all Scripture is suitable for teaching). And it has nothing to do with mothers-in-law, either. I have learned to leave some subjects alone.

First, this verse teaches us that Peter had a house. I had never thought about that before. We often view the disciples as being homeless. We might assume that Peter, being a fisherman, lived at sea. The fact was that Peter had roots. He had a real home, with a roof and all, in which to sleep at night. His home even had furniture. This should remind us that the disciples were real people, just like you and me.

Second, we see that Peter had a mother-in-law (and, no, I'm still not doing any mother-in-law jokes). But in order to have a mother-in-law, Peter must have had a wife. I hadn't necessarily seen him that way, either, until I studied this verse. And, who knows, if he had a wife, perhaps Peter even had children. We don't know this from the Scriptures, but that certainly would have been a part of the cultural expectation for most husbands and wives.

So, what's my point? Well, if you and I fail to see Peter and the rest of the disciples as real people, just like you and me—with families, jobs, responsibilities, and even

mothers-in-law—then I think we are missing a very important lesson about their sacrifice. In order to serve Christ,
Peter gave up more than just a fishing boat. He didn't just
walk away from the family business, even though that, in
and of itself, was huge. Peter gave up spending nights
with his wife, perhaps his children, and, yes, even his
mother-in-law.

The disciples gave up much so that they might follow
Christ. I don't believe God calls us to sacrifice our families
for ministry. This was a unique launch of the church. But
one question Peter's sacrifice encourages me to ask is:
What are you and I willing to sacrifice?

Prayer: God, thank You for the sacrifices You made for
me. Help me be willing to follow You wherever You lead.
Reflect: Spend a moment reflecting on the sacrifices
of the disciples in helping establish the church we
love today.

46 Rooster Crowing

Immediately the rooster crowed a second time. Then Peter remembered the word Jesus had spoken to him: "Before the rooster crows twice you will disown me three times." And he broke down and wept.

—MARK 14:72 NIV

Please don't fail to see beyond the initial truth of this familiar story. There is so much to this story, and it has been studied for years, but I think there may be even more than we see at first glance.

Yes, this is a story about humility. It is a story about standing tall for Jesus, about being unashamed of the Gospel of Christ. It reminds us of our own frailties as we watch Peter, a man full of faith, struggle with fear and doubt. Peter, the first to proclaim the foundational belief that Jesus is the Messiah and the Son of God (Matthew 16:18), has stumbled. And we see fully his humanity.

Yes, this is a story about the suffering and death Christ experienced for you and me. One of His closest disciples, perhaps the only one who dared come this far with Him, denies that he ever knew Him. Jesus would die alone.

Yes, this story reminds us of restoration and forgiveness. We read later in Scripture that Jesus brings Peter back into full fellowship with Him. Peter, obviously broken by the experience, is restored into a loving relationship with his Savior (John 21:15-19). We see from this that Christ stands ready and eager to forgive us when we fail Him.

But I want you to also see the power of God in this story. Imagine for a moment the city that day. I would suppose there was more than just one rooster, wouldn't you? And, yet God apparently controlled the mouth of every rooster until Peter had denied Him three times.

What difference does that make? It points to the fact that God will command all His creation to mold us into who He wants us to be. God uses everything He has to make us the kind of people He can bless.

Peter was never the same because God kept a rooster from crowing. Watch for God today to affect the circumstances around you to change your life forever.

Prayer: God, surely I underestimate all You do for me and the lengths You will go to make me Your disciple.
Reflect: Spend a few moments thinking about the creation around you. Look at the sky, the trees, and the animals you encounter today. Let creation remind you of the power of God.

47 | I Want to Be Famous

But, "Let him who boasts boast in the Lord." For it is not the one who commends himself who is approved, but the one whom the Lord commends.

—2 CORINTHIANS 10:17-18 NIV

"Daddy, did you ever want to be famous?"

That was the question my 10-year-old son once asked. It was an honest question requiring an honest answer. As a normal, healthy little boy, my son has often watched superstar basketball players and touchdown catching football heroes and wondered what it would be like to achieve their success. I heard him running down the halls of our house, ball in hand, pretending to be the next Peyton Manning.

There is nothing wrong with wanting to be successful in life. I also don't think it is healthy to desire to fail. But as I thought about my child's question, I realized my answer needed to be one that would help him grow spiritually.

I told him how my goal at one time was to be the President of the United States. I shared with him how I had thought I might like to be the CEO of a major Fortune 500 company and be chauffeured to and from work each day. I also told him how I had even once thought I might become a famous movie star.

Those dreams were gone, I told my son. They were gone mainly because the practicality of them had passed long ago. Even more, though, my goals became much more important as I matured over the years.

My goals may be smaller in terms of personal worldly success, but my aims are so much higher. I want to be loved most by those who know me best. And I have set my sights on nothing less than seeing Jesus face-to-face and being found in Him!

Famous? Yes, I want to be famous. I want to be one of the chosen, the redeemed, and one of the precious ones whose name is written in the Book of Life!

How about you? Did you ever want to be famous?

Prayer: God, thank You for helping me become famous with You.

Reflect: What did you dream of doing when you were younger? What is your greatest aim today as you think about your future?

48 Smarty Pants

For now we see only a reflection as in a mirror; then we shall see face to face. Now I know in part; then I shall know fully, even as I am fully known.

—1 CORINTHIANS 13:12 NIV

Someday, they are going to call you "smarty pants." Yep, it's true. One day they will.

God promises you will one day know fully just as you are now fully known by Him. Everything will be made understandable to you. The fog will be lifted from your eyes, and you will see clearly. When we, the children of God, get to Heaven, we will all rejoice in the knowledge we receive. All our questions are going to be answered.

I don't know about you, but I have more questions than answers sometimes. Why does a parent abuse a little child? Why do some couples struggle with infertility? Why is there so much hatred and racism? Why must so much of our nightly news be devoted to murder? Why is human trafficking a thing? Why did God allow snakes to survive the flood?

No doubt, you have your own unanswered questions.

There are questions whose answers we cannot grasp in our current finite minds. The most brilliant minds of our day have no real truths to give on so many subjects. Our world is full of heartache and disease that seem to have no meaning.

One day, those who have personally, by faith, accepted Christ as their Savior will be brought into the throne room of God, and we will have revealed to us God's mystery of life. We will understand His ways. We shall know for sure that His ways were right and that He knew what He was doing every time. We will see that His plans for our lives were directly proportional to the infinite depth of His love for us.

You and I will have the answers we so desperately need.

Hang on, dear brother. Keep trusting, fellow future smarty pants. Our day of knowledge will come.

Prayer: Lord, thank You that I won't always struggle for answers. Help me trust You until I am fully known.

Reflect: Add to the questions I listed previously. What are some unanswered questions you have for God?

49 Showing Honor

Remember your leaders, who spoke the word of God to you. Consider the outcome of their way of life and imitate their faith.

—HEBREWS 13:7 NIV

I grew up in the church. I have often heard people like me talk about having had "a drug problem" during their childhood. We were drugged—well, dragged, to be precise—to church on Sunday morning, Sunday night, and Wednesday night. My family was in church whenever the doors were open. Still, when I got to college I wandered from my devotion to Christ. I never denounced Him, and I attended church most Sundays, but I certainly wasn't growing as a Christian.

I was 24 years old when my pastor began to challenge me. He was a powerful, deep-hearted preacher of the Word of God. As many of my toes as he stomped on, one might have expected me to skip church even more, but there was a sincerity in his preaching that I just couldn't miss. I found myself, once again, with "a drug problem," only this time I—not my parents—was dragging myself to church. Pastor Dennis challenged me to commit myself to deeper spiritual growth. I wanted to imitate his faith in Christ.

Have you ever had such an inspiration? Is there someone in your life who helped you grow as a Christian? Is there one person, or several, in whom you could see

Christ working and it made you want to be like them? Maybe it was a parent, pastor, teacher, or even some Christian you never even knew, but whose writings inspired you.

Brother, if you can think of someone, would you do me a favor? Let them know. Tell them what a blessing they were or are in your life. Your encouragement may be just what they need to keep spreading the Good News. Your encouragement is likely deserved, and giving it is the right way to honor them.

Then, if you really want to honor them, invest in someone else's life like they invested in yours. Become a spiritual role model yourself. Disciple another believer. That is what building the Kingdom of God is all about. Each of us reaches another, and, together, we all become more like Christ.

Prayer: God, thank You for the people who have helped me become the man I am today.

Reflect: This exercise is a healthy one to build into a discipline in your life. Make a list of people who have invested in you through the years and find ways to honor them.

50 Enjoy Life with Your Wife

Enjoy life with your wife, whom you love, all the days of this meaningless life that God has given you under the sun—all your meaningless days. For this is your lot in life and in your toilsome labor under the sun.

—ECCLESIASTES 9:9 NIV

Solomon was the wisest man of all time. In his search for the meaning of life and for the real pleasures of this world, he gave us this advice: Enjoy life with your wife.

Solomon had many wives and many lovers, too. In fact, he had all the so-called pleasures of the world at his command. He had the ability to order up anything that his mind could conceive. In the end, however, he found that God's way, two people committed to each other for a lifetime, was the most excellent way. Perhaps that is why Solomon wrote Song of Songs as a brilliant tribute to the wife of his youth.

When I was in the business world, my wife and I had the privilege of working together. We got to see each other throughout the day. We had to interact on a business level continuously. At the time, our boys were still living at home, and life was sometimes hectic. Still, there was no more precious time than when the two of us had time alone, leaving the world behind, and we could focus on our love for each other. Our marriage was fueled by these special times.

These days, as empty nesters, we have more time alone together than we did when we were raising our boys. And, thankfully, we still enjoy each other's company. I'm convinced that the energy we invested in our marriage in the hectic days is what protected and preserved our marriage for these days.

Dear brother, if you are married, praise God for your spouse. Ask for God's richest blessings upon them, and that He will help you cherish them with all your heart. Celebrate the gift of life and marriage together. Commit to one person, forever. And if you, like Solomon, have made mistakes, learn from them as Solomon did. From this day forward, find pleasures in life from the simple, yet complex, gift that God has given you: your spouse.

Prayer: God, thank You for my wife and for the life we have together. Help me love her more.
Reflect: Take some time this week to write your spouse a love letter. What are some of the things that you might say?

51 Key Holder

I will give you the keys of the kingdom of heaven;
whatever you bind on earth will be bound in
heaven, and whatever you loose on earth will be
loosed in heaven.

—MATTHEW 16:19 NIV

When our oldest son turned 11 years old and reached middle school, we gave him his own key to the house. We worked less than a mile from home and had the flexibility to come and go, so we allowed him to go home some afternoons and wait for us to get off work. To be honest, it was a huge step for us in trust (even harder for my wife), but we wanted to test the prospect of giving him more authority later.

It was amazing to watch his reaction. There was a certain sense of pride in him when he realized he had been given this authority. I suspect that he would not have done anything wrong simply because he was so honored by, and grateful for, the freedom.

Have you ever heard someone jokingly say, "Well, he can't go too far because I've got the keys"? When you hold the keys, you have access, even a certain amount of control.

Jesus said He would give us the keys to Heaven. Can you imagine all that that truth means? It means we have access to Heaven. My son had access to our house that his friends did not have to theirs. If you know Jesus as your Savior, then you have access to God's Home that others may not yet have (hopefully, we are trying to help them find a set of keys).

The keys to Heaven also indicate that we have a certain amount of control. The life you live right now is determining your future rewards in Heaven. You have the keys to bind for yourself treasures in Heaven, "where moths and rust cannot destroy" (Matthew 6:20 NLT). Are you using your keys to enrich your Heavenly fortune?

Finally, the keys to Heaven indicate that you belong to the family of God, and all the benefits of being a family member belong to you. The day my son got his keys, he knew he was an important part of our home. Certainly, he was before, but with keys in hand, he knew that he was a bona fide, key holding member of the family (he never started helping with the mortgage payments, but that's another story).

If you are a follower of Christ, then you hold the keys to Heaven. Doesn't that make you feel special?

Prayer: God, thank You for handing me the keys!
Reflect: Think for a moment about those who have entrusted you with keys—literal or metaphorical. They have extended trust to you. How does that make you feel?

52 He Bears *All*

No temptation has overtaken you except what is
common to mankind. And God is faithful; he will
not let you be tempted beyond what you can bear.
But when you are tempted, he will also provide a
way out so that you can endure it.

—1 CORINTHIANS 10:13 NIV

Throughout my life there have been well-meaning
Christians who have told me that God will not put more
pressure, problems, and trials on us than we can bear.
Some would have us believe that God, being a God of
love, will only allow us to experience the stress of life up
to our ability to handle it. This simply does not hold true to
Scripture. In fact, the totality of Scripture seems to teach
the opposite.

Today's verse *does* say that God will not allow us to
be "tempted" beyond what we can bear and that He will
always provide us a way out of temptation so that we will
not sin against Him. Perhaps this is where the confusion
arises. But this verse is about temptation, not trials.

What I read in the Bible are biblical characters, heroes
of the faith, who received more burdens than they could
handle on their own. Consider Elijah. After hearing that
Jezebel was out to kill him, Elijah hid in a cave and asked
God to take his life (1 Kings 19). Moses got to a serious
point of frustration in his ministry, and his father-in-law
had to advise him to seek help (Exodus 18).

There are times when even the most mature believers face situations and circumstances that they just cannot handle. But that is why God's "strength is made perfect in weakness" (2 Corinthians 12:9 NKJV). It is why "He must increase, but I must decrease" (John 3:30 CSB). That is why "He gives strength to the weary and increases the power of the weak" (Isaiah 40:29 NIV).

God wants us to cast all our cares on Him because He cares for us. Jesus said we can do nothing without abiding in Him (John 15:5 NIV). In 2 Corinthians 1, Paul even indicates that when we can't handle what's before us, it forces us to rely not on ourselves but on God.

Life is tough. It is even unbearable at times. And, of course, that is why we need a Savior.

If you are feeling in over your head today, the answer may not be to find more strength in yourself or muster more courage. The power you need might be found down on your knees—in prayer.

Prayer: God, thank You that I don't have to go through this life alone. You are willing to carry the burdens I can't handle.

Reflect: Have you heard that statement that God won't put more on you than you can bear? Have there been times in your life when you simply couldn't hold up to the weight of stress?

53 Pick Up Your Mat

Then Jesus said to him, "Get up! Pick up your mat and walk."

—JOHN 5:8 NIV

In order to appreciate the value of Jesus's command in today's verse, you really need to think about the culture of the day. Today, although many of us may feel we don't do enough, there are limited opportunities for the physically handicapped to work, be cared for, and lead productive lives. In Christ's time on earth, the handicapped were basically guaranteed a life of poverty. They lived off the handouts they could obtain from begging.

In this instance, the man had been crippled for a long time. Probably the only possessions he had were the clothes on his back and the mat on which he lay. His existence was pitiable. There was no cure for what ailed him (except Jesus), and even if there were, he certainly couldn't have afforded it.

Jesus had sympathy for the man, and, with the spoken word, the man was healed. Jesus told him to get up, take his mat, and walk. Obviously, this was a gift greater than anything money could have bought the man.

It prompts me to ask an important question, however. What are you holding on to today?

This paralytic was holding on to his mat. It had surely become a treasured possession to him. He slept on it, rested on it, and watched the world pass by on it. He couldn't have imagined facing the day without it. Jesus tells him to pick it up and walk. When Jesus was finished with the man, he didn't need the mat anymore. It would take faith to trust Jesus and attempt to walk, but the victory was worth it all.

What would Jesus tell you to pick up today? Are you resting on your church membership? Are you trusting in your bank account? Are you drowning in your sorrow? Are you moping about the setbacks of your life? Are you suffering from the sin that has wrecked everything around you? Do you fail to commit to God because you are afraid that He can't accept you?

Dear brother, whatever ails you, I believe Jesus would say, "Pick up your mat and walk!" Trust Him with what you now trust the most. Permit Him to see you through the difficult days of life. Allow Him to carry your burdens, strengthen your walk, and brighten your hope for the future. He is still the Miracle Maker, and He can still heal a broken heart.

Prayer: Lord, thank You for the healing You provide us when we trust in You.

Reflect: Where do you feel "paralyzed" in your life today? Make a note of it here and keep praying. God is listening.

54 Victory in Jesus

But you belong to God, my dear children. You have already won a victory over those people, because the Spirit who lives in you is greater than the spirit who lives in the world.

—1 JOHN 4:4 NLT

Brother, what are you afraid of these days? Why has the world shaken your trust? Don't you know that you are a child of the King and that everything is under His control?

Sometimes, believers can look like everyone else when it comes to how we deal with the pressures of life. We tend to allow stress to be our motivator instead of relying on God's light to direct our paths. Christians should have a power that the world cannot measure. We have been bought with the precious blood of our Savior, Jesus Christ.

Not long ago, during one of those extremely hectic days (ever have one of those?), I saw myself getting caught up in the fast-paced rat race of life. I was moody, sarcastic, and easily angered, all because the world was tossing more at me than I could handle on my own. I turned around at my desk and my eyes were attracted to a plaque that was hanging on my wall. It simply read: Wise Men Still Seek Him!

Of course they do.

I realized that I was fighting this battle all on my own. I don't have to win the victories of my life. My battle is technically over. I am already on the winning team. My life is now centered on building up for myself eternal treasures. I am now in the process of decorating my Heavenly mansion (I'm going with a gray/taupe schematic).

Suddenly, my disposition changed. The problems were still there, but I had a new perspective. As I reflected on who God is and who I am with Him, instead of drowning in my problems, I was able to walk away from my desk and say it had been a great day.

Do you need a new perspective? Is life getting you down? Focus on the victory you have in Jesus. Remember, you are on the winning team.

Prayer: God, thank You for the eternal victory I have in You!

Reflect: If you know the song, why not sing (or hum) a couple of stanzas of "Victory in Jesus"? How does this make you feel?

55 Love One Another

This is the message we have heard from the beginning: We should love one another.

—1 JOHN 3:11 NLT

Jesus said we should love one another as He has loved us.

Unless, of course, they pull their car out in front of you or are in the express lane with more than 15 items. Unless they took your parking place, forgot your birthday, or are fans of a rival sports team.

I could go on with more serious conditions:

Unless they don't share your political views. Unless they belong to a different religion. Unless they are the person who hurt you most. Unless they hurt someone you love.

Add your own qualifier. You get the idea.

We should ask ourselves, however, if there can be an exception to the law of Christ so simply stated in three words: Love one another.

Hopefully, you understand that there are no reasons for us to refuse to love one another. Someone may be aggravating, and they may even make us righteously angry—but still, we must love them.

I realize this is hard to accept, but consider the life of Christ. As He walked this earth, He loved the unloving. He loved those to whom no love was shown. Did He always commend their deeds? No, of course not. If the person was a sinner, Jesus said, "Go and sin no more." But Jesus always offered His love. His love was not based on the person's actions, but on the simple fact that the character of Christ is love.

God Himself is love, and we who call ourselves followers of Christ are challenged to be likewise. Brothers, there is a lost world that needs to see the love of Christ. In the letter from which today's verse is quoted, John also writes that we must not love just in word and speech, but in action and in truth. This world needs a heaping helping of demonstrated love.

Is your life a picture of Christ's love? Are you "loving one another"? Would others who know you well agree?

Prayer: God, help me love even those who are most difficult to love.

Reflect: If you had to be honest, who are the most difficult people for you to love? Now, imagine you had to tangibly prove that you love them. Does that change your answer?

56 Daddy's Boy

See how very much our Father loves us, for he calls us his children, and that is what we are! But the people who belong to this world don't recognize that we are God's children because they don't know him.

—1 JOHN 3:1 NLT

Years ago, I was asked to give the keynote speech for my son's elementary school graduation. Of course, I agreed to do it, mostly because my son was in the program. It wasn't my highest earning speaking gig (I got nothing), but it might have been one of my greatest honors.

When I arrived at the school, my son's classmates didn't know why I was there. They knew I was a dad, but I wasn't anyone special until I stood up to speak. To the fifth graders, I immediately became someone important. I was suddenly a big deal.

Even though I wasn't anyone to be impressed by, they were impressed.

As my son discovered this fact, he wanted me to recognize him. He didn't want anyone failing to realize who he was and who I was to him. Not only was it an honor for me, but it held a few bragging rights for my son. At least for this moment in time, my son thought it was good to be my son.

Do you feel that way about being a child of God?

Think about it. You are God's child, a family member of the Creator and Sustainer of the Universe! Your Heavenly Father owns the cattle on a thousand hills. He directs the path of sunlight and sets the stars in place. Your Dad establishes kingdoms and authorities and tells the rain when to fall from the sky. Your family is wealthy. In fact, your Father owns it all.

So many people have no clue what a blessing it is to be a part of Christ, but you and I do. We should never stop grinning because of what we have in Him.

If you are a part of the family of God, say *Amen*.

Prayer: God, You make me proud to be Your son. Thank You for loving me.
Reflect: Think for a moment of one of the proudest moments of your life. Now, imagine how proud God must have been of you that day.

57 Frosted Flakes

Then the Lord said to Moses, "I will rain down bread from heaven for you. The people are to go out each day and gather enough for that day."

—EXODUS 16:4 NIV

The Israelites might have been appropriately called "The Grumblers." Led out of Egypt to escape persecution and find the Promised Land, God's children never really seemed pleased with their new surroundings. Yet, God cared for them. Whenever they were hungry, God gave them something to eat.

Every morning, thin flakes, like frost, would cover the ground (I always like to think of this as the world's first breakfast cereal). The bread was called *manna*, and we are told it was like toasted bread and sweet like honey (proving God does care about the taste buds he placed in our bodies).

The people could only gather enough manna for one day's feeding. If they gathered too much, it would spoil. The next morning, except on the Sabbath, they would go out and gather more.

God did this miracle to demonstrate to His people that He could supply all their needs. Are you hungry? God can provide. Do you need something to eat? God is able. Every single day.

Despite the miracle, do you think the Israelites were originally surprised that God could cover the ground with "frosted flakes" every morning? Of course, they were. It was truly "new every morning."

What are you praying for right now? Do you believe that God can provide it?

Let me ask you to simply trust that God can and will provide. Now, He may provide in His way. The Israelites may have wanted Froot Loops and gotten Frosted Flakes, but God did satisfy their need.

Ask God to meet your needs, trust Him to do it, and then wait for His answer. God is still in the manna business today. After all, He is the Bread of Life.

Prayer: God, thank You for Your provision. Help me trust You more.

Reflect: List a few current needs you have in your life. Ask God to provide them in His way and in His timing.

58 Honesty

Honest scales and balances belong to the LORD; all the weights in the bag are of his making.

—PROVERBS 16:11 NIV

Honesty is still a respected virtue. At least, I hope it is.

When I worked in the meat department of a grocery store in high school, we had to delete the weight of the packaging before we put a price on the meat. The idea was that you need to be paying for the meat and not the packaging. Imagine paying $5.99 (probably $1.99 at the time) a pound for plastic wrap and Styrofoam. At that price, give me pork chops (or cheap steaks).

When you buy something by the pound, you want the scales to be accurate. In the meat department, we were required to regularly check the accuracy of the machine. It was even regulated by the government. I hope grocery stores today do the same thing.

Honesty in the sale of meat is important. Honesty in business and government is important.

But honesty is even more important in relationships. My children always knew they would get in far less trouble if they were honest with me than if they lied and I found out later. In my marriage, my wife needs to know that she can trust me no matter what. She needs me to be honest with her, just as I need her to be honest with me.

For a relationship to be strong, there needs to be trust, and that is only attained in honesty (suddenly, I have a Barry Manilow tune stuck in my head).

Did you know that honesty comes from God? God is the Creator of truth. He *is* truth. It is God who began the idea that meat should be sold accurately and that children and adults shouldn't lie to each other.

As I consider our world today, I think we need more men and women who will stand for truth. We need to protect the virtue of honesty. We need to be defenders of truth. And, ultimately, if we want honesty in our world, then we need to introduce people to the Maker of honesty.

Oh, how we need the Lord.

Prayer: Lord, help me be honest in all that I do and in every relationship in my life.

Reflect: Where are some places you see that we need more honesty? What can believers do to help encourage a culture of honesty?

59 Ewok

But those who seemed to be the leaders—I say this because it makes no difference to me what they were; God does not judge by outward appearances—those leaders, I say, made no new suggestions to me.

—GALATIANS 2:6 GNT

Years ago, my family went white water rafting for the first time. We were going on a rough part of the river, so we wanted to be sure we knew what we were doing. There were about eight guides, one for each raft, and my family would be in our own raft with our own guide.

When one of the guides stood up to give instructions to the group, we knew instantly that he was the guide we wanted. He was good looking, strong, and clean-cut. We wanted our first white water experience to be perfect, and we were certain it would be with Joe (not his real name) as our guide.

We soon found out that Joe was not our guide. Our guide was Ewok. That's his real name. Ewok's name said a lot about him. He had long hair down the middle of his back, sort of cut in a mohawk style. There were only a few inches of his body that were not covered with tattoos. He and I would probably never share the same tailor. Our first impression of Ewok was that we did not want him to be our guide.

(I apologize for that now. I've grown as a person since then.)

We got out into the water, and one of our first experiences was with Joe, the first guide. He rowed over to our raft, asked us if we knew what was "lousy," then proceeded to splash us with very cold river water. After the third time it began to wreak havoc on the contacts in my eyes. Joe turned out to be somewhat of a jerk.

Ewok, on the other hand, was a true gentleman. Once, when we got hung up on a rock, he was quick to remedy the problem safely. We found out later he was the most experienced guide on the river that day. He took great care of our family.

After we got back into our car that day, I used this experience to teach my family (and myself) a valuable lesson. We had misjudged Ewok based solely on appearance. He deserved better from us from the beginning.

God does not judge by outward appearances (1 Samuel 16:7 NIV). Aren't you glad?

Prayer: God, thank You for viewing me not from my actions or my appearance, but by my heart.
Reflect: Thank God He doesn't judge the way we sometimes do.

> But we do not belong to those who shrink back and are destroyed, but to those who have faith and are saved.

—HEBREWS 10:39 NIV

My mother is not tall. All her children passed her in height early in life. I must say, however, that what she lacks in physical stature she more than makes up for in the stature of her character.

Once, one of our boys (I won't say which one, in case my mother reads this) asked me, "Has Nanny always been that short, or did she shrink when she got old?" First, I told him my mother was not that old. Second, I said she has been that short for as long as I can remember.

I have heard, however, that it is a biological fact that people tend to shrink in height as they get older. I'm pretty sure I've shrunk at least an inch. When the writer of Hebrews encouraged believers not to "shrink back," though, he wasn't talking about physical height. He was talking about spiritual height.

I have seen it time and time again. People start out strong but sometimes finish weak. I can't tell you how many people have gotten excited about "doing the church thing." They attend every time the doors are open. They volunteer for ministries. They want a position. They are the up-and-coming among the Christian circles, and then, after a few months, or at best a few years, they seldom enter the church doors.

It could be due to a break in a relationship, a bad experience in church, or they just lost their fervor. They started strong but shrunk back.

I have also learned that often the threat of an illness or a disease will bring them back. Or a financial reversal comes their way, and they call fervently upon the Lord again. Their faithfulness tends to come based on the circumstances of their lives at the time.

Brother, may we never shrink back. May we not lose the devotion to Christ that we had when we came to salvation. May we never fail to give Jesus His proper place—first place—in our lives.

Regardless of any changes to your physical stature in the years to come, where Christ is concerned, I urge you to make a commitment today: *Don't shrink back.*

Prayer: God, give me the strength to stand strong and finish well.

Reflect: Think for a moment about people who once had such passion for Christ, but now you hardly see them in church. Pray about whether you should reach out to them.

61 Enoch Walked with God

By faith Enoch was taken from this life, so that he did not experience death: "He could not be found, because God had taken him away." For before he was taken, he was commended as one who pleased God. And without faith it is impossible to please God, because anyone who comes to him must believe that he exists and that he rewards those who earnestly seek him.

—HEBREWS 11:5-6 NIV

The life of Enoch can be found early in the book of Genesis. According to the Scripture, after Enoch became a father, he began to walk with God. I don't know exactly what this means, but as he was walking with God, apparently Enoch disappeared from the earth. He did not die. He did not run away. He simply disappeared. God had taken him to his Heavenly Home. Enoch's faith gave him quick access to Heaven.

Enoch is an example of faith because he was an early committed follower of God. I have often wondered if Enoch began to fully comprehend the relationship God wanted with him after he became a father.

Before I had my first child, I knew all the answers. I watched others raising their kids and identified the mistakes they were making. I didn't have a full grasp of parenting, though, until I became a parent. I now know the importance of fathering and how much I wanted to develop a close relationship with my boys. I also better understand that my boys were watching my relationship with God and likely modeling it, too.

Enoch became a father, and then he put his complete faith in God. Perhaps you have needed some visible example of what faith in God means. Perhaps Enoch did, as well. Look at the life of Enoch and try to identify with him. Here was a man who loved his children, saw that God loved him likewise, and decided that God was worthy of his complete faith and obedience.

Use Enoch as your model today. Enoch saw the faith and obedience his children placed in him and knew this was exactly what God was looking for from him.

Prayer: God, thank You for the examples of men of the Bible and in my own life, who teach me what it is like to walk with God.

Reflect: Are you a father? What have your children—or a relative's children—taught you about God?

62 Three Temptations All Men Face

For everything in the world—the lust of the flesh, the lust of the eyes, and the pride of life—comes not from the Father but from the world.

—1 JOHN 2:16 NIV

Do you share my struggle with temptations? I am convinced that the temptations of most, if not all, men can be found within the three listed in this verse.

We are tempted with the lust of our flesh. I cannot speak for women as this is a men's devotional. The temptation of lust would have to be among our greatest struggles. Could I be interested in pornography if I allowed myself to be? Of course, I could. The temptation of lust is strong for all of us. To live a life of purity and keep from sinning, I must flee this temptation.

We are tempted by the lust of our eyes. I would be better off if I didn't know some things existed. I seem to want what I do not have. I covet my neighbor's goods. If he gets a new car, it makes me want a new car. Obviously, it is not wrong to have a new car, but that should not become an object of my complete attention and affection. It is wrong, I would even say a sin, to lack contentment in the things God has allowed me to have.

And, finally, the temptation to be prideful, to make ourselves bigger than life. Every man wants to be respected. If we are not careful, however, we will turn this natural desire into foolish pride and temptation. It is easy for us to want to assume glory and leave God completely out of the victories of life. The temptation to look good is so strong that it often keeps us from achieving all God would call us to do.

These three temptations can prevent us from achieving all God wants for us as His children. As we grow as disciples, we must be careful to avoid these temptations as we concentrate on following Jesus more closely.

Prayer: God, protect me from falling into the trap of these temptations.

Reflect: Do you agree with my assessment? Do many of the temptations with which men struggle fall into the categories of this verse? What else would you add?

Jesus Knows Your Name

"How do you know me?" Nathanael asked. Jesus
answered, "I saw you while you were still under the
fig tree before Philip called you."

—JOHN 1:48 NIV

Jesus knows your name. Isn't that a blessing? I'm told He
even counts the hairs on your head.

Nathanael was a person who just had to know how
and why. He was the type of person who got to the
bottom of a matter. He asked great questions. When
Jesus recognized Nathanael, it prompted him to inquire of
Jesus, "How do you know me?" I don't think he was being
rude. He was just being Nathanael.

He reminds me, quite frankly, of my own son
Nathaniel. Have you ever met someone in public, and,
when they called you by name, you wondered how they
knew you? If a waiter, say, called Nathaniel by name, my
son would (politely, I hope) ask, "How do you know me?"

Of course, we know how Jesus knew the Nathanael
of John's Gospel. He knew him just as He knows you and
me. He was there at our conception. He was there at our
birth. He was there in the delivery room, anxious to see
the smiles on everyone's face as mom and dad and the
grandparents welcomed us into this world. Jesus watched
as the earth prepared for our arrival. He counted down
the days until we were born. In fact, He was there before

time was created. He was there with the Creator, giving His approval to our lives.

The reason Christ was so eager to obey His Father and to suffer and die on the Cross was that He was already intimately involved with us. He had already invested His time in knowing the person we would one day become.

And Jesus is so interested in us today and longs for us to come to know and love Him because He has a vested interest. Jesus is committed to us because He has known us before we had the capacity to know Him.

Jesus knew Nathanael, and He knows you and me. He has known us for a long time. Jesus knows your name. Shouldn't that make you happy today?

Prayer: God, thank You for knowing me so well and yet loving me so much.
Reflect: Think for a moment about how well God knows you. Doesn't it make you want to be more honest with Him in your prayers?

64 Doubts Are Normal

Immediately Jesus reached out his hand and caught him. "You of little faith," he said, "why did you doubt?"

—MATTHEW 14:31 NIV

I was once asked to rappel off a tall training wall as a part of a leadership class. We were on a military base. I put on all the safety gear, went to the edge of the wall, and turned around. The next step was the scary part: the actual jump. Everything was okay after that. Well, maybe not. I still had to get down, but the initial fear was over.

Now that I know that rappelling can be safely done, even by me, one would think I was ready to do it again. The fact is, however, that I would likely have to overcome that same fear all over again. Even though I know rappelling is safe, I couldn't bring myself to do it again.

Life is that way sometimes, isn't it? We know who God is, that He can do what He says He can and that He will. What is more difficult is seeing that played out every day. That is especially true when the storms of life come our way. No matter how many times He delivers us, the next time the wind blows may cause us to doubt again.

Peter is a good example of this principle. Peter's belief of Jesus as the Messiah was the foundation for the church. Peter left his fishing business to follow Christ. Peter cut off the Roman soldier's ear when they tried to arrest Jesus. Peter was capable of great faith.

It certainly took faith to step out of that boat. Jesus called to him from the boat, and Peter volunteered to come to Jesus. Jesus didn't even ask him to. Think of the amazing faith it must have taken to make that first step onto the water (maybe you have seen someone walk on water, but I haven't). But when the wind picked up a bit, Peter was ready to doubt. He started to sink. He couldn't see Christ from the fear of this world.

Are there ever times when you can't see what God is doing because the circumstances of life are bigger than you can handle? I think Jesus might say to you (and me) what He said to Peter: "You of little faith, why did you doubt?"

If you and I have our eyes on Jesus, we have nothing to fear.

Prayer: God, thank You for the times You reach out to catch me when I'm doubting.
Reflect: If you had been Peter and Jesus told you to come to Him on the water, do you think you would have stepped out of the boat? Or would you have stayed in the boat with the other disciples?

65 Silver and Gold—*Not*

Then Peter said, "Silver or gold I do not have, but what I do have I give you. In the name of Jesus Christ of Nazareth, walk."

—ACTS 3:6 NIV

A friend of mine went through a period of years in which he played in many golf tournaments. He also loves the Lord and always tries to serve Him. My friend keeps on trying, but, for some reason, he never gets better than second place in golf.

One day, I told him I was sorry he couldn't place first. I figured it was a big deal to him or else he wouldn't keep trying. I'm sure he would love to win, but I really appreciated his response.

He said, "Silver or gold I do not have, but what I have I give you." He quoted this text to remind me that although he doesn't have first place trophies, he does have an eternal crown. Amen.

Peter had left a profitable fishing business to follow Christ. In biblical days, to own a boat meant you had at least some stature in the business community. Peter gave up his own interest to become a disciple of Christ.

After Christ had ascended into Heaven, Peter continued spreading the Gospel. When Peter and John came upon a crippled beggar at the temple gate, they literally had no money to give the man. They, too, were now living from handout to handout, depending on the goodness of God to feed His disciples. What they did have to offer the crippled man, however, was worth far more than any coins. Peter offered the man the salvation of Jesus Christ and the power of His healing. The man would never be the same again. And neither would Peter.

Let me ask you something. What do you have to offer? Perhaps you are quite wealthy. Perhaps you are poor in a monetary sense. Do you have what will last forever?

Silver and gold you may not have, but, more important, do you have Jesus?

Prayer: God, thank You that with You I have all I could ever need or want.
Reflect: How content are you these days with the things God has allowed you to have?

66 Unity

As a prisoner for the Lord, then, I urge you to live
a life worthy of the calling you have received. Be
completely humble and gentle; be patient, bearing
with one another in love. Make every effort to keep
the unity of the Spirit through the bond of peace.

—EPHESIANS 4:1-3 NIV

In my experience, conflict or disunity usually develops
because we want what we want. That's true whether in
interpersonal relationships or even in a church context.
Most conflict has more to do with what we want than
anything else. Worship battles, for example, are seldom
about anything biblical. They happen because I like certain
music and don't like other music.

Paul's recipe to resolve most conflicts was simple. Put
Jesus first. Place the interests of others ahead of your own.
You can apply that principle to most relationship conflicts.

We want what we want, so one key to healthy conflict
is to consider the other person's perspective. When we
put ourselves in the other person's shoes we will find that
most conflicts don't even need to happen. We have got to
be willing to drop many things that simply don't matter.

Let me give you an example from my marriage. Cheryl's organizational skills are phenomenal except in one
area: the kitchen cabinets. I'm the cook in our family, so
I want the kitchen organized for efficiency. For Cheryl, as

long as the cabinet door closes, she doesn't care how the things are arranged behind the door.

When we got married, she would put a bowl in the cabinet and close the door. I would open the door and see chaos. It drove me crazy. How long would it take to stack the bowls? Soon, I began to complain about it and cause needless conflict that would only hurt our relationship—and she still didn't stack the bowls.

I let it go. All these years later, you know what: She now stacks the bowls without me even prompting her.

The reality is that most disagreements won't go away without some form of conflict. Healthy relationships have conflict, and the partners learn to deal with it. But let's make sure the conflict we have isn't based solely on our own selfishness, and let's consider the bigger goal of unity in all relationships.

Prayer: Lord, help me not get hung up in my relationships on selfish things that only matter to me.

Reflect: Be honest. Are there conflicts in your life that you just need to drop?

67 Obedient Witness

"And now, compelled by the Spirit, I am going
to Jerusalem, not knowing what will happen to
me there. I only know that in every city the Holy
Spirit warns me that prison and hardships are
facing me."

—ACTS 20:22-23 NIV

Paul was apparently well-known in Jewish circles. After he
became a Christian, he felt compelled by the Holy Spirit
to go to Jerusalem. This was not a safe city for Paul to
visit. At the time, the Jews were growing in their rejection of Christ. Paul's fervor for telling the Good News of
Christ made him a marked man in the city at the center of
Jewish leadership. Still, Paul followed the Lord's lead and
set out for Jerusalem.

What I find interesting is that Paul went knowing he
was going to face "prison and hardships." He knew life
was going to be difficult if he obeyed God. And yet, he
obeyed. He obeyed when he knew that a cold, dark jail
cell awaited him. He obeyed when he knew that beatings
awaited him. He obeyed when he knew rejection and
hatred awaited him. Paul obeyed even when he knew the
comforts of life were going to be taken from him.

People today still live with the faith of Paul. I have been
told there is more Christian persecution around the world
these days than at any other time in human history.

The question that begs to be asked is this: Would you and I obey God if we knew for sure that doing so would make life uncomfortable, even dangerous? I don't know about you, but I like the comforts of my home. I like having neighbors and friends around who embrace my faith. It is nice to live in an area of the world where I can freely attend church.

I hope you and I never have to face the level of persecution others do, but we should remember that in order to be fully obedient to God, we may have to get out of our comfort zones. We may have to do things we wouldn't necessarily pick for ourselves and go places we wouldn't normally go. And we might have to witness to our coworkers, neighbors, or friends, even if they reject our witness.

Prayer: God, give me the courage to be a witness for You today.

Reflect: Who has God placed in your path that, as far as you know, has no relationship with Christ? Consider how you might be a witness to them.

68 Adversity in the Center of God's Will

Saul told his son Jonathan and all the attendants to kill David.

—1 SAMUEL 19:1 NIV

If you recall the story of King David, one day he was tending sheep and God called him to be a king. He didn't ask to be king, but God said he was the one. He turned out to be a good king. The Bible tells us that David had a heart modeled after God's heart.

Yet even though David was God's chosen one, during the days when David had been anointed to be king but hadn't yet assumed the role, David was chased by King Saul. In today's verse, we learn that King Saul was even trying to kill David.

David ended up hiding, often all alone (at such times, it is likely he wrote many of the Psalms). David was God's choice for king, yet he was placed in such incredible adversity.

What does this tell us?

What it says to me is that sometimes God's will for us will find us in the middle of trials in life. More important, I have learned that I cannot determine whether I am in the middle of God's will based on whether my life is peaceful at the time. The fact that I have difficulties in life is no indication that I am not being obedient to God.

Think about Abraham, who faced the trial of leaving his homeland; Moses, who wandered in the wilderness for 40 years; or Joseph, who was sold into slavery before he was used by God to save a nation. Nehemiah had to fight off naysayers to rebuild the walls of Jerusalem. Daniel was thrown into a lion's den. All these great servants of God faced persecution, heartache, and trials beyond most of our imaginations. Yet, all of them, during the adversity, were right where God wanted them to be. They were in the center of His will.

We would all like for life to be peaceful and stress free. Of course, we can have inner peace in the middle of the storms of life, but God has not promised us a life free of problems. We can stand perfectly within His will and still face plenty of adversity. In fact, it is often part of the process God uses to make us more like Jesus.

Prayer: God, help me trust in You regardless of the circumstances of my life.

Reflect: Think about what you have learned and how your character has been shaped by past trials and difficult circumstances.

> Your love has given me great joy and encouragement, because you, brother, have refreshed the hearts of the Lord's people.

> —PHILEMON 1:7 NIV

There was a man in the church where I last pastored who embodies this Bible verse. He "refreshes the people." Every time I saw him on Sunday, he encouraged me in some way. It could be about the message I preached, the clothes I was wearing, or just a simple pat on the back to tell me he loved me. If I had an exceptionally stressful week, I made sure our paths crossed for a pick-me-up.

Of course, I was the pastor, and some people like to encourage their pastor, but I wasn't this man's only mission. I saw him encouraging others in the same way. He had a reputation for blessing people.

Philemon was apparently that kind of guy. In this letter to him, Paul praises Philemon for his work in the church. Philemon must have been a source of encouragement. Whenever Paul thought of Philemon, it gave him a warm feeling. Perhaps thinking of Philemon and those like him who serve in love helped keep Paul from losing his mind while locked up in a cold prison cell. Paul needed the encouragement that came from knowing there were still people who cared whether he lived or died.

We all need that type of encouragement. Regardless of how mature in our faith we become, we need people around to help keep our spirits strong. We need someone we can trust, someone who can bring a smile to our face, and someone who has our best interests at heart. Even though the Lord is our "friend who sticks closer than a brother" (Proverbs 18:24 NIV), I firmly believe God surrounds us with Christian friends to help make this fallen world a bit more tolerable.

Do you have a friend like that? Better still, are you a friend like that? Can others count on you for a kind word, a smile, or an encouraging compliment? Are you careful not to say something unless it will edify and build up the body of Christ? Will you, like Philemon, be an encouragement among the church?

May that be our prayer and goal today!

Prayer: Lord, help me be a blessing to others today.
Reflect: Who, in your life, is like Philemon or the friend from my church? Consider letting them know. They may need encouragement, too.

70 Cast Your Cares

Cast all your anxiety on him because he cares for you.

—1 PETER 5:7 NIV

According to the Bible, when we cast our cares upon the Lord, we have a promise that God will take care of us. This is a theme throughout the Scriptures. We hear it not only from Peter but also from David in the Psalms: "Cast your cares on the LORD and he will sustain you; he will never let the righteous be shaken" (Psalm 55:22 NIV).

I recall an incident years ago when I was a junior management member of a large retail operation. I was asked to put together a report to be seen by the company's senior management. Shortly after beginning the task, I realized I was in over my head. I didn't know how to do what I had been asked. I was on a deadline, and there was no one around to ask for help. One afternoon, when I was just about to give up, my immediate supervisor walked into my office and agreed to take over the project. I instantly felt a huge weight removed from my shoulders.

That's the imagery of casting our cares upon the Lord. He takes over. He initiates the next moves. He replaces our worries with His strength. He takes our faith and molds it into His victory. He sustains us so that we can face the situation knowing that He is fully in control.

This doesn't mean you don't have to do anything, but it does mean the ultimate outcome is under His control.

140 90-Day Devotional for Men

Of course, when we cast our cares upon the Lord, He expects us to leave them in His hands. I couldn't have gone back to my boss after he assumed that special project and asked for the responsibility again. My boss was in control at that point, and he would also receive praise for the report.

God wants to be responsible for your concerns, to act upon your behalf and for your good, so that He will get the glory in the victory.

Prayer: God, thank You for inviting me to cast my cares upon You and assuring me that You will sustain me.
Reflect: What are you attempting today on your own that you should trust God to help you with?

71   What's Your Story?

I want you to know, brothers, that what has happened to me has really served to advance the Gospel, so that it has become known throughout the whole imperial guard and to all the rest that my imprisonment is for Christ. And most of the brothers, having become confident in the Lord by my imprisonment, are much more bold to speak the word without fear.

—PHILIPPIANS 1:12-14 ESV

What is your story? We all have one. If I could sit with you and share coffee for an hour or two, getting to know each other, who or what would be the key markers in your life that have shaped you into the man you are today?

My father was in and out of my life when I was a child. He was an alcoholic and verbally abusive. It was not until I was an adult with my own children that he returned to the Lord. I did not realize the impact he had on me until I was in my forties. Today, that is part of my story. I have been able to sit with countless other men with similar stories and help them because of that painful part of my childhood.

I have owned a couple of businesses. I always say no one understands stress until they are responsible for the payroll of others. One business was very successful. The other not so much. It was a painful season trying to make payroll and keep the doors open. I would never want to go back to that time, but, because of it, I have sat with dozens of struggling business owners. I understand their pain. I can identify with them.

There are so many other parts of my life I could share, but the point is that God has used my story for the advancement of His mission to the people around me. Just as the Apostle Paul shared, what has happened to me has been used to advance the Gospel.

So, what is your story? Are you allowing God to use it for His good purposes in your life and in the lives of others?

Prayer: Lord, let my past be used in a way that advances the Gospel.
Reflect: What are painful parts of your life that you have tried to hide but that God may want to use for His good?

72 Committed to Christ

For the eyes of the LORD range throughout the earth to strengthen those whose hearts are fully committed to him.

—2 CHRONICLES 16:9 NIV

As a Bible study teacher and a pastor, people often come to me expressing a desire to grow in their relationship with the Lord. They want to be godly fathers, more active church members, and better people in general. They might say they want a stronger faith, a closer walk with the Lord, or a deeper prayer life. Some would say they want to grow a godlier marriage or raise their kids to walk closely with Christ.

The requests are varied, but the intent is the same. They want to be better disciples of Christ. I always applaud them for their desire, which I believe is genuine.

Unfortunately, many of those same people who express a desire for oneness with the Lord are people in whom I see a lack of commitment. I believe many of them really do want to grow in the Lord, but they either don't know how to get there, how to stay there, or how to really put forth the effort required to make their goal a reality.

If a wholehearted devotion to Christ is your goal, and you aren't there yet, may I ask you a question? What are you doing to help yourself get there?

In the Christian life, with all that Christ did for us on the Cross, you and I still have an obligation in the growth process. We are saved through our faith and by grace alone, but in order to really grow as Christians, we must commit ourselves to being discipled. Growth is a process. It is a day by day, week by week, year by year event that requires our participation.

To be a growing follower of Christ requires dedication, such as daily Bible reading and prayer. It requires a commitment to gather with a group of believers on a regular basis. It requires yielding our own will to God's will and sacrificing our plans for His perfect plan.

The good news is that God is still looking for people to bless who will follow Him with all their heart. Will you and I be found in that group?

Prayer: Lord, help me be diligent in seeking after You.
Reflect: Think for a moment about the spiritual disciplines you have in your life. Are they helping you grow in your dependence and commitment to Christ? If not, what changes do you need to make?

73 | Humble Servant

Jesus knew that the Father had put all things under his power, and that he had come from God and was returning to God; so he got up from the meal, took off his outer clothing, and wrapped a towel around his waist. After that, he poured water into a basin and began to wash his disciples' feet, drying them with the towel that was wrapped around him.

—JOHN 13:3-5 NIV

Jesus was the perfect example of servant leadership. The King of Kings washed the smelly feet of His disciples. The Creator got on His knees to show the full extent of His love. I don't quite understand that kind of love, but as I have studied this passage, I believe I have discovered why Christ might have been persuaded to humble Himself in such a way.

First, Jesus knew He had authority. In fact, God had given Him ultimate authority. So, He didn't have to fear embarrassment. God was protecting His reputation.

Do you know the power God has given you? He said you can "resist the devil, and he will flee from you" (James 4:7 NIV). He promised that "anyone who believes in Him will never be put to shame" (Romans 10:11 NIV). He declared that you and I "can do all things through Christ who strengthens [us]" (Philippians 4:13 NJKV). You and I, the children of God, have power through Christ.

Second, Jesus knew where He came from. He came from God. Christ was there at the formation of the heavens and the earth. He gave His approval when God spoke the universe into existence. He already knew the feeling of sitting at the right hand of God. Jesus's permanent address is Heaven.

Those who have accepted Christ have also come from God. We are new creations. We are joint heirs with Christ. We are aliens, fellow pilgrims in a foreign land. This world is not our Home. We are God's children, not born under the law, but born again into grace.

Third, Jesus knew where He was going. He knew God would not forsake Him but would come to take Him Home again.

You and I have that promise even today. Christ is waiting for the Father to give the signal, then He will come to get God's children. Those of us who are saved will be going Home!

We can be servants because we know God's power is in us, we know we belong to Him, and we know that one day we will be going Home.

Prayer: God, help me be a humble servant, following Your example.
Reflect: Think about situations where you may have the opportunity to serve people, even people who might not have the power, influence, or resources you have.

74 Smelly Feet

For he knew who was going to betray him, and that was why he said not everyone was clean. When he had finished washing their feet, he put on his clothes and returned to his place.

—JOHN 13:11-12 NIV

When we look at Christ's incredible act of service of washing His disciples' feet, something very profound jumps out at me. Jesus washed 24 feet. He washed 12 pairs of feet. Twelve disciples. Twelve sets of feet. Twelve (disciples) times two (two feet for each disciple), equals 24.

Are you impressed with my math abilities?

I'm sure you know how to count, too, but I want to illustrate a point about Christ that literally blows my mind.

Jesus washed the feet of every disciple, including Judas, whom He already knew was about to betray Him. Do you catch that? Judas Iscariot, who would soon betray Jesus by selling His location to the Roman soldiers, got his feet washed along with the rest of the disciples.

I am somewhat of a germophobe, but I can imagine washing my wife's feet. I can imagine washing the feet of our two boys. I can even imagine, if I absolutely had to, washing the feet of a close friend (if I have one reading this, don't ask). But, with everything inside me, I can't imagine washing the smelly feet of an enemy. Can you?

Perhaps you are one of those people I have encountered who simply has a hard time believing a holy God could love someone like you. Brother, look at the example of the servant leader, Jesus Christ. He does not discriminate in dispensing His love. He does not qualify His love by your actions or inactions.

Jesus washed the feet of Judas, to whom the Gospel was available, just as it was to the rest of the disciples. Judas rejected Christ, but Christ did not reject Judas.

And Christ has not rejected you.

Prayer: God, thank You for being a humble servant and for providing an example for me to strive to live by.
Reflect: Think of someone who has hurt you. I'm not going to ask you to wash their feet, but could you say a prayer for them?

75 Give Thanks in Everything

Give thanks in all circumstances; for this is God's will for you in Christ Jesus.

—1 THESSALONIANS 5:18 NIV

The Word of God says to "give thanks in all circumstances." That is a plain and simple, easy-to-understand command, and, if we choose to, we will know exactly what to do with it. It is similar to the verse that directs us to "do everything without grumbling or arguing" (Philippians 2:14 NIV). There is no grey area of interpretation. We are to thank God for everything.

We might be tempted to reply to God that life is not always easy. Life is full of sorrow, full of disappointments and pain. There are trials that test our faith. We have situations that bring fear and worry daily. There is heartache and distress all around us. We witness the breaking of relationships in the home, devastating financial situations, and people we love suffering from poor health. This world is full of chaos and sin, and, Lord, people dishonor Your name.

How can we possibly give thanks in *all* circumstances?

I do not believe God is asking us to give thanks for all those bad things I listed; I don't believe He is sadistic. Evil is nothing to rejoice over.

God is encouraging a longer-term perspective than that. He is telling us we can give thanks in all circumstances because He has all circumstances under His control.

I can almost hear God's reply as He looks upon our seemingly desperate situations, "Do not fear. While from your perspective things look troubled, from my perspective everything is okay. I have it all under control. Go ahead, you can truly give thanks."

God does, indeed, have our lives within His hands. He is sovereign, and we, His children, are a part of the master plan He is working. He sees the end. He sees the victory. He sees the promise. He provides the hope.

Through faith in Him, we can give thanks in all circumstances. Not because everything seems to be going our way, but because everything *is* going *His* way. God is in control.

Prayer: God, thank You for having everything under control so that I can be thankful.

Reflect: How is your attitude of gratitude lately? Spend a couple minutes and list some things for which you are extremely thankful.

76 Steadfast and Immovable

Therefore, my beloved brethren, be steadfast, immovable, always abounding in the work of the Lord, knowing that your labor is not in vain in the Lord.

—1 CORINTHIANS 15:58 NKJV

As a pastor, when I read this verse, I see a three-part sermon outline. Corinth was a port city with a strong economy and an emphasis on the arts and architecture. With its significant resources came all the temptations of wealth and prosperity. In modern terms, it was a very worldly city. Paul encouraged the Corinthian believers about the type of life they should live in such a setting.

He told them to be *steadfast*. The literal meaning of the word is "to sit." It does not mean to do nothing, but the connotation is one of being permanently grounded. When everyone else is turning away from their faith, you remain seated with your Lord.

Paul also said to be *immovable*. This is a very similar word, but the addition here seems to imply that Paul expected the Corinthians to be subjected to strong temptations. Try as we might to obey God's commands, we can still be distracted. Paul emphasizes that we are not to be moved when those times come. We remain faithful amid the flirtation of the world.

Finally, Paul tells the Corinthian believers they should *always abound in the work of the Lord*. I think Paul knew there would be a natural inclination, while the Corinthians remained steadfast and immovable, to remove themselves from the world completely. But we have been called to make disciples. We are told to be in the world but not of the world. We cannot escape to our Christian bunkers. The Gospel compels us to be light in the middle of darkness.

Paul concludes by sharing the reason behind his encouragement. We remain faithful, knowing that what we do for God will be used and rewarded. This is not a "name it and claim it" verse. This is a promise that God never wastes an opportunity to bless and reward obedience. Either in this life or the life to come, God will use our works, which are done for His glory, to richly enhance our life and the lives of those around us.

Prayer: Lord, help me remain seated firmly in Your presence, doing Your work even when the world is drifting from You.

Reflect: In what areas of your life might you have drifted from God's plans and desires? How will you remain steadfast and immovable in the days ahead?

What He Has

"But we only have five loaves and two fish here,"
they said to him.

—MATTHEW 14:17 CSB

The story of the feeding of the 5,000 always reminds
me of the problem the disciples faced. It is often my own
problem in trying to follow Christ, especially during periods of uncertainty.

The people were hungry. Jesus had compassion for
them, so He told the disciples, "You give them something
to eat."

The disciples gave an honest, calculated, reasonable, and
even responsible reply. When they surveyed the landscape—
thousands of people—they literally only found five loaves
and two fish. That's it. No more. Send the people home.

They weren't trying to be difficult or disobedient. It
wasn't even that they had no faith. These were the closest followers of Jesus. They had left everything to follow
Him. They were simply responding based on what they
could see. And based on that—end of story. Nothing else
to do here.

But see, their problem was in their reply.

Notice what they said to Jesus: "But we only have . . ."

It's true that if the focus were on them, the story
would've pretty much been over. If they were the ones in
charge of this operation, the people would have had to go
away hungry. If all they had was what they could see, they

would have been in trouble. It's perfectly logical that if they had to rely on their own abilities or on their own resources, one boy gets to finish his lunch, but everyone else better stop at Chick-fil-A on the way home.

Yet, equally true, *Jesus* had told them to feed the people. *He* had given them the command. *He* had sent them to complete the mission. And where God sends His people, He supplies their needs.

When the focus was on Jesus, the people were fed, and they picked up 12 baskets of leftovers.

And here is the challenge for us today. When we focus on what we have and what we can do, we'll be disappointed. We may become scared. We see what we don't have far more clearly than what *He* is offering us.

But when we focus on what He has and what He can do, we gain a new perspective. We are encouraged. We are comforted, even with all the seemingly impossible obstacles ahead. And we have more courage to approach them.

Prayer: God, help me remember that You will never send me on a mission (or even to face a day) without having already prepared my way.
Reflect: In what area of your life do you struggle most to accept that God's provision will be enough?

78 Marriage Ground Rules

"In your anger do not sin": Do not let the sun go down while you are still angry, and do not give the devil a foothold.

—EPHESIANS 4:26-27 NIV

As a pastor, I frequently encounter couples at odds with each other. I often find that their current disagreement began long before with the buildup of smaller, unresolved conflicts. For example, if a husband says something to his wife and she receives it as unkind, even if his intent wasn't to be hurtful, that action, left unresolved, could result in a long-term, serious division for them.

I encourage couples to operate with some ground rules in their marriage based on biblical principles. My wife and I have these for our marriage.

One rule is to keep short accounts. In order to keep from building conflict, this rule leads my wife and me to have a couple of practices. First, we try to never go to bed angry. I have learned that if my wife goes to bed angry, she tends to wake up angrier.

This sometimes means we need to stay up later to resolve an issue. At least, we will agree to let go of the anger before going to sleep. As the spiritual leader in my home, my job is to enforce this rule. This usually means that I need to be willing to swallow my pride, admit where I was wrong, and seek forgiveness so we can get some sleep.

Second, we never leave the house while angry. Escaping a problem will never solve it. It only leads to resentment and deeper anger. This rule also means we don't sleep on the couch unless we are sick. Escaping promotes a false idea that there is a way out of the problem other than pushing through conflict to solve it together.

Finally, in keeping short accounts, when anger is stirred, it must be discussed in love. No issue can be swept under the rug. We try to keep in mind that building a healthy marriage is our goal. Meeting that goal requires the two of us to become one. Anger only gets in the way of living God's will for our marriage.

Marriage is hard. Protecting it should be the goal of all believers.

Prayer: Lord, protect my marriage, especially from those things that we can't control.

Reflect: Considering your marriage and the differences between you and your wife, what ground rules do you need to keep the marriage strong?

79 Greener Grass

The day for building your walls will come, the day for extending your boundaries.

—MICAH 7:11 NIV

Driving down a country road one day, I saw something that reminded me of an important principle in life, especially in the Christian life. I passed a field full of cows grazing. Close to the road was a large metal gate covering the entrance to the field.

At the gate was a little calf, trying desperately to get through the gate to the other side of the fence. This calf must have seen some grass that looked better outside the fence. In the meantime, all the other cows appeared to patiently graze among the grass within the fence. I wonder what would have happened if the calf had gotten through the gate?

For one thing, it would have been in danger of getting hit by a car, but I wondered if it would miss its mother when the time came for milk. That calf reminded me of how I am at times. I often think that the grass looks greener on the other side; better than what we've got.

It's hard sometimes for me to be patient with where I am in life. In that discontentment, I often find myself testing the boundaries God has given me and trying to create my own opportunities. Of course, I find out later that what God had for me was best. Have you also learned some hard lessons like that?

Have you found out that what you thought you so desperately wanted wasn't worth it once you got it? Thank God for boundaries. Thank God for all the trouble and heartache He has kept me from because I have surely brought enough on myself as I have stepped outside of His perfect will.

One of my missions raising sons was to teach them not to always look for the greener grass but to be content where God has them at the time. I didn't encourage them to stop dreaming or taking risks, but I did urge them to be satisfied with where God has them at any given time. If God brings about those dreams in His sovereignty, they will certainly be even more appreciated.

I suspect, however, that my boys have had to learn this lesson as I am still learning it: through experience as I discover over and over that God's way is best.

Prayer: Lord, help me find my contentment in life in You!
Reflect: Where in your life are you feeling a sense of discontentment? Ask yourself: Will I be okay with God if He doesn't change things as I want Him to?

80 Three Truths

But put on the Lord Jesus Christ, and make no provision for the flesh, to fulfill its lusts.

—ROMANS 13:14 NKJV

I see three truths God may be trying to teach us through His Word today.

First, we are to "put on the Lord Jesus Christ." When we became Christians, we received access into the mysteries of God, namely Jesus Christ. We now have the heart of Christ living in us through the promised Holy Spirit. We now have access to understand (not yet fully) the mind of God.

Still, we must "put on the Lord Jesus Christ." This is a daily process as we meditate on His Word, pray, and experience fellowship with other believers. Jesus lives in us, but we must choose to reflect on Jesus in us.

The second truth is found in the phrase, "and make no provision for the flesh." Our flesh is the old habits and ways we develop in our life that operates outside of God's plan for us. The flesh is all we are and do apart from fully relying on God to meet our needs.

This verse tells us not to make any "provision for the flesh." Elsewhere, the Bible tells us, "do not give the devil a foothold" (Ephesians 4:27 NIV). The key is to keep our heart and mind on Jesus. When we are fully surrendered to Christ in our heart and mind, temptation will have no power in our life. We will be able to reject sin.

Finally, by God's grace, when we "put on the Lord Jesus Christ" and "make no provision for the flesh," we will not "*fulfill its* lusts." Whose lust? The lust of the flesh.

Lust, as it is used here, is basically wanting something you shouldn't have. We all have certain needs for unconditional love, acceptance, appreciation, respect, and self-worth. When we attempt to get them outside of Christ, we are operating from our flesh. The desire to get these needs met outside of Christ is called lust.

One of the best ways to get rid of sin and stagnation in your Christian walk is to recognize the power of lust. We need to recognize that lust will lead us astray and take us from God's perfect plan.

If you are attempting to find satisfaction in any place except the Lord Jesus Christ, you are settling for far less than the best God has to offer.

Prayer: Dear God, shine the light of Your Truth for us in this verse and let it change the way we live in *You*.

Reflect: Where is the place of greatest temptation for you? In what ways are you battling the flesh?

81 An Ugly Hat

No discipline seems pleasant at the time, but painful. Later on, however, it produces a harvest of righteousness and peace for those who have been trained by it.

—HEBREWS 12:11 NIV

"This is the coolest hat I've ever had!"

That was the comment my son made about a hat he'd found a thrift store. You would have to see it to clearly understand, but it was the ugliest hat I had ever seen. There was a new trend among his teenage friends to find the ugliest hat and wear it proudly. The most popular hats were mesh back style (farmer's hats) that were old, worn out, and would usually be found hanging on a back porch somewhere after many years of hard use. My son's hat had a blue bill and white mesh. On the front of the cap was the cartoon character, Tweety Bird. The hat must have just barely escaped being thrown away on several occasions due to its age and wear. My son, however, now thinks it's the "coolest hat" he's ever had.

When he told me this, the Lord gave me a great teaching moment (when boys get to the age of 15, there are fewer and fewer of these times). I asked him, "Jeremy, if I would have told you a year ago that this would be your favorite hat today, what would you have thought?" "I would have thought you were crazy," he said. "So,"

I continued, "in your wildest imagination, last year you could have never seen yourself liking this hat."

I went on to explain that this is the way it is sometimes when I need to discipline him or give him advice. At the time, it may not make sense to him. He may not understand what I am doing, but one day, he would look back and see that my logic was pretty good.

It also served as a good teaching moment for me. Many times, God has something for me to endure that I cannot understand, and there seems to be no good benefit for the trial that I am enduring. In time, however, the good that God is seeking in my life will be more apparent. During the trial, I will simply have to trust that God knows what He is doing.

Prayer: Thank You, God, for teaching me, through the simple things of life, the truths of Your Word.
Reflect: What are you learning from others these days? If you have children, what has God taught you as you've tried to teach them?

82 Prayer Distraction

Then he returned to his disciples and found them sleeping. "Could you men not keep watch with me for one hour?" he asked Peter.

—MATTHEW 26:40 NIV

Do you think if Jesus ever invited you to pray with Him for an hour that you could stay awake?

Jesus was about to endure the Cross. He knew the pain ahead was going to be horrendous. He asked His disciples to pray with Him, but they fell asleep.

Why is it that having an effective prayer life is really such a struggle?

Jesus certainly understood and practiced the power of prayer. I want us to consider the major obstacle in prayer. It is simply that Satan doesn't want you and me to have good prayer lives.

I was preparing to preach on prayer once, so I wanted to pray about it. If you are going to preach on prayer (or any subject, for that matter), you should probably pray about it. For some reason, as hard as I tried, I couldn't seem to get the words to come out of my mouth. I've been a Christian for some 30 years now, and the one area where I continue to struggle is in my prayer life.

I know it's not where it needs to be. Why is that? I used the illustration of the disciples today because I wanted to show that I am not alone in my struggle. Perhaps you have the same obstacles to prayer in your life.

You should know that it is no accident that we struggle in our prayer life. Satan has a scheme. He is working on a time limited master plan. Satan loves to distract our prayer life. Do you know why? Because prayer is serious business and Satan knows it.

Satan doesn't mind if you are busy with church work, but, when we pray, things start to happen. When Jesus prayed, "heaven was opened and the Holy Spirit descended on him" (Luke 3:21-22 NIV). Heaven responded when Jesus prayed.

If you and I ever get serious about prayer, we will see Heaven open when we pray, too. And the Devil knows it. He would do anything to keep us from praying.

If we want to learn to be like Jesus, we will have to be aware of the Devil's efforts to keep us from praying.

Prayer: Lord, teach me to pray.
Reflect: What is the biggest distraction or obstacle that keeps you from praying more?

83 Check Your Passion

Jesus gave them this answer: "Very truly I tell you, the Son can do nothing by himself; he can do only what he sees his Father doing, because whatever the Father does the Son also does.

—JOHN 5:19 NIV

Jesus was not a robot. In His humanity, He had given up His Kingship and taken on the qualities of man. The Bible says, "he made himself nothing . . . he humbled himself" (Philippians 2:7-8 NIV). Jesus chose to follow His Father and do what His Father commanded Him to do. So, when we are striving to be like Jesus, we make a choice to take on His characteristics, just as Jesus assumed the characteristics of God. He chose not to sin because God had no sin.

When we consider the passion of Jesus, we know then that Jesus had a passion for the things in which God displayed passion. Jesus got excited about the things God got excited about. Jesus was passionate about protecting God's name, church, and people. He was passionate about being a Savior. That was surely what gave Him the determination to endure the Cross. Finally, Jesus was passionate about getting rid of sin. He desperately wanted victory over the Devil.

And Jesus's passion paid off for you and me. He did protect God's name and God's people. He completed the assignment God called Him to. Jesus fought the war over sin and death. He won. The battle is over. Satan is defeated. Jesus will one day eradicate sin when He joins us permanently with our Heavenly Father.

Are you passionate enough about the things of God that you will finish the work He has called you to do? Will you finish your task? Will you be found faithful?

Let me give you a little suggestion. If you have no zeal for the things of God and His Kingdom, you will usually fail at what He calls you to do. We tend to best complete those things for which we are most passionate.

Prayer: Lord, give me a passion for the things of You and Your glory.
Reflect: Check your passion and see if it lines up with Jesus.

. . . and find out what pleases the Lord.

—EPHESIANS 5:10 NIV

Throughout my life, I've tried to get my life back to the blank-piece-of-paper stage.

Let me explain.

In visiting with a friend of mine once, he gave me a simple illustration that I began implementing in my life. This friend had been a mentor of mine for several years. He had walked through many of the places I have walked.

He is just a few years older than me, but he's farther along in life than I am. He's been married a few years longer. His children are a few years older. He was in business a few years before me. He's been a Christian a few years longer. All this works to my advantage whenever I seek direction from him for my life.

I was explaining that I was at one of those "trying to discover God's will" points in my life. His advice was something like, "Maybe you need to start with a blank piece of paper and give God ample space to plan out the rest of your life. Make yourself completely available to Him."

That made a lot of sense to me. I left our meeting, however, with a very probing question for myself. Do I have a blank piece of paper?

It wasn't that I didn't have any paper in the house. With two boys in school, we had plenty of paper. My friend was talking in a spiritual sense. Had I given God a "blank page" with which to plan out my life? Or, was I trying to help God write the plans? Was I writing plans for God, and then asking Him to bless them, or was I truly allowing Him to shape every major direction I took in my life?

After self-examination, I had to be honest. I couldn't say that I had offered God a blank piece of paper. I certainly wanted to follow His lead, but I think my page was loaded with some of my own agenda items.

Here's how I responded to the realization. I took a couple of days just to get away from everything. I tried to be all alone. I spent time fasting and praying. When I was through, at least for that moment, my page was completely blank. Then, I offered it back to God.

Prayer: Lord, help me as I endeavor to present You with a blank page.
Reflect: Ask yourself: Have I given God a blank page for my life?

85 Lavished Grace

In him we have redemption through his blood, the forgiveness of sins, in accordance with the riches of God's grace, that he lavished on us.

—EPHESIANS 1:7-8 NIV

Paul was deep. His writings reflect a keen mind. He could have fit into any intellectual discussion, probably about any issue. No wonder God wanted Paul to write so much of the New Testament. Sometimes, I must read and reread a passage Paul has written, and without the Holy Spirit's help, I don't think I would ever come close to understanding it.

But Paul is simple here. He says that we are saved by God's grace because of what Jesus did for us on the Cross. Then, he goes on to say that God did it in His wisdom and understanding. We were lost and in need of a Savior. God loved us, and, recognizing that need, He sent His Son to die on our behalf. He extended His grace to us, and, when He did, He held nothing back. God gave us His very best when He gave us Jesus.

But I have another way I choose to see this text. I make it personal.

Paul says God "lavished" grace on us. I like the word, *lavished*. When I read it, I get a visual image from real life. It has to do with one of my favorite meals—steak and a baked potato.

I like my potatoes a certain way. Loaded with butter. When I eat a baked potato, everyone in my family knows I want my potato "lavished" with butter. I want it packed with butter until it is oozing out all over.

And that's a crude way of illustrating that God doesn't give us a "little bit of grace." Paul says he lavishes grace on us.

Do you know why God can meet all your needs, according to His riches in Christ Jesus? Because He had advance notice of the outcome, He knows how the story will end, and so He has lavished His grace upon you to meet you at your point of need.

If you have Jesus, you will never lack for grace.

Prayer: God, thank You that through Your wisdom and understanding, You lavish us with grace.
Reflect: How do you feel when you think about the amount of grace God has given you?

And Jesus grew in wisdom and stature, and in favor with God and man.

—LUKE 2:52 NIV

"Jesus grew." I love the imagery of Jesus growing from the baby in a manger into a man. One day in Heaven, I hope to hear more of what His life growing up was like.

Jesus grew in wisdom. He committed Himself to studying God's Word and learning from those with more knowledge of the Scripture than He had. He was devoted to memorizing Scripture and applying God's truth to His daily life. He learned to put God's wisdom to use for good.

Jesus grew in stature. He became (even more so) a man of His word. He earned respect through a godly example and through "Christlike" living. He became a man that God could depend on to carry out His master plan.

He grew in God's favor. He worked to please God. Now, keep in mind, Jesus never sinned, but He was tempted to, and He had the human ability to. He simply chose *not* to sin. He obeyed God. He placed His total faith in God the Father. Remember, Jesus said, "the Son can do nothing by himself; he can do only what he sees his Father doing" (John 5:19 NIV). That is faith, and, as the Bible says, it is impossible to please God without faith.

Finally, He grew in favor with men. I want to assure you that it is impossible to please everyone. If you live a committed Christian life, you will cause opposition. Jesus

Himself brought about opposition, but among those He called brother, Jesus sought to be at peace. Jesus forgave easily, judged slowly, accepted graciously, and loved generously. Jesus loved His neighbor as Himself. He wasn't a pushover with no backbone, and He didn't condone sin, but He did love the sinner and tell them with love the wonderful way to the Kingdom of God.

How about joining with me in trying to grow like Jesus?

Prayer: Lord, help me grow in wisdom, stature, and in favor with God and man.

Reflect: Think about what it must have been like to be Jesus growing up as a boy. What images of Him come to mind? How do you picture Him at that time of his life?

87

Only by Prayer

He replied, "This kind can come out only by prayer."

—MARK 9:29 NIV

The people had brought a demon possessed boy to Jesus's disciples for help in deliverance. The disciples had tried to drive out the demon. They had watched Jesus do it so many times before. It didn't seem like something they couldn't do when they were with Jesus. Jesus had said, "If you have faith the size of a mustard seed, you will tell this mountain, 'Move from here to there,' and it will move" (Matthew 17:20 CSB).

On this occasion, everyone was watching, too. What would people think if they weren't able to get rid of this evil spirit? People might think less of them. They might say, "You're not really His disciples," or "Look at you, you can't do anything by yourself," or "Where's your faith?"

The disciples' reputation was on the line.

Jesus took care of the problem, and then, humbly and privately, the disciples asked Jesus, "Why couldn't we drive it out?" (Mark 9:28 NIV). It was a fair question, wouldn't you agree? Why couldn't they perform what seemed to be a simple task? Why couldn't they do what they had been trained to do? What was the cause of their failure?

Jesus had a simple answer. "This kind," Jesus said, "can come out only by prayer."

That leads me to ask a sobering question. What are you going through today that can only come out by prayer?

I'm sure you are very spiritual. You may have great biblical knowledge from years of study. You may even know your pastor. You are probably a committed follower of Christ. You have a testimony. You could even have the "good attendance" pin for going to church. You are likely an example for other men to follow. You even give God the glory for your life. You are surely capable of doing *His* work.

But, you see, this kind can come out only by prayer.

Today, whatever it is, no matter what people might think or say, turn it over to the Lord. Let Him know you need Him. Thank Him for all He has done for you before but tell Him you need Him once again. Tell Him you realize that apart from Him, you can do *nothing*.

Turn it over to God today, in prayer.

Prayer: God, I give You my situation and my life to do as only You can.

Reflect: Do you have any stories or experiences in which you know prayer made the difference?

88

The Promised Land

Trust in the LORD and do good; dwell in the land and enjoy safe pasture.

—PSALM 37:3 NIV

Put on your creative hat for a moment. I want you to imagine that you are a cow or a sheep. Feel free to even let out a *moo* and a *baa*, just to get into the role.

Now, imagine you have been on this land all your life, grazing, sleeping, running, and drinking water. One day, suddenly, out of nowhere it seems, a wolf appears. The wolf kills three of your friends. The next day, the wolf appears again and gets four more friends. This continues every day for a week. You begin to get scared.

At the same time, the grass you have been eating begins to dry up all around you. You have a hard time finding anything to eat. Your children (the calves or lambs) are beginning to question you. You are worried about where your next meal will come from.

Then, a disease hits the flock or herd. Half the animals are wiped out in a single month. Tragedy has hit. You don't know what to do.

Then, everything changes.

One day, a great day indeed, a wealthy farmer purchases you and your kids. He takes you to a new field. The grass is greener than you ever imagined, and there is plenty of hay in the barns if it ever dries out. There is a master veterinarian right on the property in case anyone gets sick. The grounds are monitored day and night by ranch hands, and you are under their constant protection. And each night, before the sun goes down, every animal gets a massage and rubdown (Is that stretching your imagination too far?).

Now, read that verse again: "Trust in the Lord and do good; dwell in the land and enjoy safe pasture."

Can you start to apply the truths of what God has done for you to my corny little story? If you are a child of God, you will find His safety, His care, and His love all around you.

And you might want to quit imagining you are an animal now. People are beginning to stare.

Prayer: Lord, thank You for the safe pastures You provide for me.
Reflect: What images come to your mind when you read about God's care for us as the Good Shepherd?

You are the salt of the earth. But if the salt loses its saltiness, how can it be made salty again? It is no longer good for anything, except to be thrown out and trampled underfoot.

—MATTHEW 5:13 NIV

How salty are you?

My wife and I have an eight-year-old Yorkipoo dog. Other than barking a bit too much, she is super sweet. One of her favorite things to do is sit in my lap and lick my hand or arm. We used to have another Yorkie who did the same thing. Both dogs tend to lick me more than they lick my wife. I once asked a veterinarian why that was the case. He simply said, "You must be the saltier one."

Salt is a preservative and a flavoring. It is used for practical purposes and to enhance flavor. Both are incredibly important today, as they were in biblical days. That's the physical aspect of salt.

Applying that to our spiritual life, as believers, we are to help preserve the world around us. We are to be peacemakers and unity builders. We are to encourage forgiveness and help settle conflicts. We are to be agents and vessels of God's grace.

We are also to add flavor to the world. Who doesn't like to be around a person filled with pure joy? How do you feel around someone who truly loves you—not for what you can do for them, but just for being who you are?

Isn't it comforting to be around people with a positive outlook on life, who fill the world with a sense of hope?

In terms of physicality, my veterinarian was probably right. I am saltier than my wife. To be candid, though, in the spiritual sense, my wife is probably the saltier one. I need to work on that.

And I think the way to be saltier is to spend more time hanging out with the Salt Maker. When I begin my day in God's Word and in prayer, I am literally saltier for the world around me. I have more patience to share. I have more love to give. I'm filled with hope and encouragement.

Let's strive today to be salt. Our world needs it more than ever.

Prayer: Lord, allow me to be saltier for my world today.
Reflect: How "flavorful" are you being to the world around you today? Are you adding a seasoning that enhances the lives of the people in your life?

90 Never Be Thirsty Again

Jesus answered, "Everyone who drinks this water will be thirsty again."

—JOHN 4:13 NIV

Let me remind you of the story. Jesus was on His way to Galilee. John writes that Jesus "had to go through Samaria" (John 4:4 NIV). It would have been very strange for a Jew, like Jesus, to go through Samaria. The Samaritans, who were half Jew and half Gentile, were hated by most Jews. Jesus not only went through Samaria, but He made a planned pit stop to draw water from Jacob's well.

At the well, Jesus met a Samaritan woman. Again, this was a strange event because Jewish men were not to speak to women in public, especially not a Samaritan woman. And not one with such a past as this woman, who had five prior husbands and was now living with a man who was not her husband. To complicate matters further, Jesus asked the woman for a drink. Talk about radical for the day.

Jesus then made a statement that seems even stranger than His being in Samaria. He said that anyone who drinks "this water" will thirst again. Can you say "Duh"? Thank You, Jesus, for that startling revelation (please don't read this as disrespectful; I am attempting to make a point). If you didn't understand Jesus's intent, you would begin to think He was simply stating the obvious.

When Jesus talked about *this water*, He was not talking about the water she was drawing from the well. As was often the case when Jesus spoke, He used a metaphor and was actually speaking of the Samaritan woman's heart. He was basically saying, "Anyone who drinks the spiritual water you've been drinking will thirst again." In other words, if you are satisfying the thirst of your heart in the world, then your heart will soon be thirsty again.

If you are finding your fulfillment in money, fame, or any other worldly pleasure, then, shortly after the fun, you will be thirsty again. Jesus offered this woman Living Water. He was offering Himself, the cure for spiritual thirst.

Brother, may I ask you: *Are you thirsty*? Are you trying to find your happiness in life through the things of the world but finding out you just cannot become satisfied? "This water" will never cure your thirst for good. Maybe you need to draw from the well that contains Living Water.

Jesus is the only real cure for the thirst of life.

Prayer: God, help me fill my every need and desire with You.
Reflect: Based on where you are seeking to find fulfillment in life, are you going to keep getting thirsty?

Verse Index

About the Author

Ron Edmondson is a pastor, church leadership consultant, and author. His ministry encourages leaders and churches to realize their fullest potential for the Kingdom. For years, Ron has also invested in helping men succeed as husbands, fathers, and friends. His favorite roles, however, are those of a husband, father, and grandfather.

Ron and his wife, Cheryl, have two grown sons and two wonderful daughters-in-law, all serving in ministry. They live in the Nashville area and enjoy loving on their precious granddaughters.

Ron blogs regularly at RonEdmondson.com and is found on all forms of social media.